SALES
SCRIPTS
THAT $ELL

SALES SCRIPTS THAT $ELL

SECOND EDITION

Teri Gamble, Ph.D.
and Michael Gamble, Ph.D.

AMACOM

American Management Association

New York • Atlanta • Brussels • Chicago • Mexico City • San Francisco
Shanghai • Tokyo • Toronto • Washington, D.C.

Special discounts on bulk quantities of AMACOM books are
available to corporations, professional associations, and other
organizations. For details, contact Special Sales Department,
AMACOM, a division of American Management Association,
1601 Broadway, New York, NY 10019.
Tel: 212-903-8316. Fax: 212-903-8083.
E-mail: specialsls@amanet.org
Website: www.amacombooks.org/go/specialsales
To view all AMACOM titles go to: www.amacombooks.org

The quote on page 163 is from DEATH OF A SALESMAN by Arthur
Miller. Copyright 1949, renewed © 1977 by Arthur Miller. Used by
permission of Viking Penguin, a division of Penguin Books USA Inc.

Library of Congress Cataloging-in-Publication Data

Gamble, Teri Kwal.
    Sales scripts that sell! / Teri Gamble and Michael Gamble.—
2nd ed.
        Includes bibliographical references and index.
        ISBN-13 978-0-8144-7421-1
        ISBN-10: 0-8144-7421-7
        1. Selling.   I. Gamble, Michael.   II. Title.

    HF5438.25.G355   2007
    658.85—dc22   2007020032

Printing number

10   9   8   7   6   5   4   3   2   1

Contents

Prologue   vii

Act I
The Groundwork

Scene 1: Why and How to Use Sales Scripts That Sell   3
Scene 2: Globalizing Sales   7
Scene 3: Technology, MEdia, and Sales   19
Scene 4: Language Success Secrets   25

Act II
Action!

Scene 1: When Using Sensible Selling   37
   Scripts to Prospect With   43
Scene 2: Controlling the Sale   69
   Scripts That Help Control the Sale   75

Act III
Tackling Roadblocks

Scene 1: Countering Objections Positively   81
   Scripts for Overcoming Objections   85
Scene 2: Handling Stalls   121
   Scripts for Handling Stalls   125

Act IV
Wrapping It Up!

Scene 1: Closing Successfully   143
   Scripts That Let You Close Successfully   147
Scene 2: Obtaining Referrals   153
   Scripts That Get You Referrals   157

Epilogue   161
Index of Scripts   165
Casting Call for More Sales Scripts That Sell   179
About the Authors   181

Prologue

Sales Scripts That Sell! is designed to give you a real selling advantage over your competition. Whether you are a beginning or seasoned sales professional, this book provides you with the words and tips you need to powertalk your way to success. As an added benefit, it will help you increase your market penetration and earn more money. No longer will you be deterred by rejection, turndowns, stalls, or maybes. Suddenly, at your fingertips and on the tip of your tongue, you will have scripts you can use to prospect, make appointments, control the sale, overcome objections, handle stalls, close sales, and get referrals.

Besides helping you avoid costly sales blunders, *Sales Scripts that Sell!* ensures that the language you use is on target, positive, and effective. Containing a multitude of solutions to the selling problems that salesforce members face and hear each day, this book is simply the most practical, professional resource available to today's sales community.

When this manual is used properly, you will have access to effective scripts that elicit new business, identify customer needs, overcome stalls and barriers, and answer objections that get in the way of closing. And it does so in an appealing and easy-to-learn format.

If you are a sales professional, you need these scripts simply because you need answers, and when you need answers, you need them right away. You do not need answers buried in a CD or DVD program or in the pages of a purely motivational sales book, or hidden with your notes from the last sales seminar you attended; you need them where you can find them. These scripts put all those important answers at your fingertips and on the tip of your tongue—where they belong.

Of course, this work was not created in a vacuum. We would like to offer sincere thanks to the following people who served on our advisory panel of professionals:

We also offer special thanks to our editors at AMACOM, including Christina Parisi, Mike Sivilli, and Bernice Pettinato.

In addition, we owe a very special debt of gratitude to our kids: Matthew Gamble, Ph.D., and Lindsay Michele, MBA, who through the years taught us more about selling and persuasion than we could imagine.

Teri Kwal Gamble, Ph.D.
Michael W. Gamble, Ph.D.

SALES
SCRIPTS
THAT $ELL

THE GROUNDWORK

Why and How to Use Sales Scripts That Sell

Cast of Characters

The Sales Star .... You
The Prospect .... Your Prospect

The Setting

All of the various places you sell, including the office, your prospect's office, in the field, in restaurants, at conventions, in the car, on the golf course, at company functions.

The Time

Right now; the present.

STAGE DIRECTIONS

Throughout the book are stage directions for using many of the scripts. They are designed to help you incorporate the scripts into your own selling presentations.

Scenes from a Sale

John reaches for the phone; he decides to go for coffee instead. Susan sits steadfastly in her car, parked in front of the office of a potential client; she sits and she sits. Alex completes a product presentation, only to find that the customer has suddenly become very busy and has to excuse herself because she is late for another appointment; he stands speechless as she leaves. Danielle agonizes for weeks negotiating a deal that never comes together.

John, Susan, Alex and Danielle represent just four of the thousands of sales professionals who fail to consummate important sales transactions every day. Why are their real opportunities transformed into missed opportunities instead? Why are their scenes from a sale all too frequently disappointing and demoralizing? The answer: They are enacting sales scenes that lead to failure rather than starring in sales scenes that lead to success. This book can change that.

We have written this book for two key reasons: (1) to provide materials that you can use to develop your selling abilities right now, and (2) to motivate you to do what you have to do if you are to produce enormous earnings for yourself and your firm. Experience shows us that after practicing the scripts contained in this book, you will handle yourself more like a winner when working in sales.

This book is a complete training manual of winning scripts that will increase your determination to succeed and your ability to find business and sell like magic. It will help you overcome "show stoppers"—words that get in the way of a sale. It will help you create pathways to success by demonstrating how to link buyer wants and seller needs.

"Where is the Magic?" You Ask?
The Magic Is in Your Words and Actions!
The Magic Is in You!

Why Use This Manual?

Our purpose is to provide you with powerful scripts you can use to increase your ability to establish rapport, build trust, bolster your confidence, answer objections, overcome sales resistance, and close transactions. No one can deny that having the words that work (scripts that add persuasive power to your sales message) at your fingertips and on the tip of your tongue will add to your sales-success ratio. Working with these scripts will allow you to be in control of the selling situation. You will learn the most effective ways of handling client or customer stalls, hesitancies, and concerns. It is indisputable that having the right answers to the most commonly raised objections will help you portray unwavering confidence and make your life as a salesperson less stressful and more rewarding.

Far too few salespeople believe they are as persuasive as they could be. Far too few salespeople believe they can sell their product or service to anyone at any time and in any place. Now you can revise that perception because you will finally have the information you need to handle each and every objection and stall that comes up during face-to-face and telephone sales calls.

How to Use This Manual

This collection of the most powerful sales scripts available is organized by category. The scripts are preceded by motivational introductions and warm-up exercises and are contained in any easy-to-carry and easy-to-use book. The format facilitates practice sessions for face-to-face calls and makes the book easy to refer to during telephone sales calls.

Each script has a title that contains a key word or two from the script itself. These titles make it easier for you to recall the various scripts as you speak to customers or clients. In addition, many of the scripts contain stage directions, which are suggestions for use and delivery. The stage directions, which appear in italics, function as would a personal coach were he or she able to stand in the wings during each selling encounter.

Note that some script material is enclosed in brackets and printed in italics. This feature instructs you to substitute data that pertain only to you and your selling situation, such as [*your company*] or the [*product/service*] you sell, or the brackets may indicate an alternate choice of words, such as [*he/she*], depending on your situation.

We suggest that as you work with the scripts, you also make notes. Underline or highlight key words and phrases that you particularly want to recall. As you interact with customers in your real-world laboratory, you will find ways to customize the scripts to meet your particular product line, locale, and clients. Add these notes to the book as well; they will also serve as a reminder of those words that are really working for you.

The information contained in each scene helps you qualify your customer, understand customer requirements, focus on your customer's attention, isolate and answer your customer's objections, ask your customer powerful selling questions, and close the sale. It does all this by helping you remember those words that get the job done. If you can close your sales more quickly, you will close more sales. If you close more sales, you'll earn more money. If you earn more money, so does your company. Answers to a multitude of objections, stalls, and questions are readily available right here. Racking your brain to come up with an answer is unnecessary. Instead of being unnerved by your customer, you can now maintain selling control and deliver line after line of powertalk.

Before we start, however, we need to talk a little about how globalization impacts selling, and about interacting with people from different cultures.

Globalizing Sales

Globalization impacts selling. With this fact at the forefront of your mind, how do you respond to the following tried-and-true advice?

"Ask questions."

"Think positive."

"Get face-to-face with prospect."

"Keep in contact."

"Help your customer feel comfortable."

"Earn your client's trust."

While these kinds of practical suggestions summarize well-known and ac-cepted sales tactics, considering the kinds of changes we're experiencing in today's world, are they still useful given a multicultural sales context? The answer is, "Yes, but. . . ." Like all of us today, sales professionals live in a mar-ketplace gone global, one that has been technologically revolutionized and now links sales reps physically, electronically, and digitally to prospects around the globe.

The global, technologically advanced village is the new context for selling. But selling to prospects in the United States, East Asia, South America, or Africa requires that you, the sales professional, use different sales styles. So does selling to persons of different ages, genders, races, or ethnicities, but more on that later. First, let's look at the role culture plays in your sales future.

Understanding Culture's Role in Selling

Different sales strategies work with clients who adhere to culturally specific criteria. Every prospect brings a set of predetermined and culturally influenced or culturally specific goals to a sales situation. Thus, selling cross-culturally requires that you become a multiculturalist, a person respectful of and engaged with others from distinctly different cultures. When selling across cultures you must pay attention to *diversity*, the recognition and valuing of difference encompassing such factors as age, gender, race, ethnicity, and religion. Enacting multiculturalism bridges cultural differences and problems that stand in the way of increased sales. So if you want to be the best salesperson *in the world*, first you must acknowledge the role culture plays.

Ask yourself these questions:

- Do I feel prepared to sell in the global village?

- Do I have the skills needed to sell to different cultures?

- Do I have the understanding and sensitivity I need to interact in communities in which the persons I sell to may look, act, and think differently than I do?

- Am I eager to embrace diversity?

Preparing to Sell Across Cultures

Assess your personal preparedness to sell effectively with persons of different cultures by labeling each of the following statements as true or false:

1. I enjoy calling on persons who are unlike me as much as persons who are like me.

2. I am equally sensitive to the concerns of all groups in our multicultural society.

3. I can tell when clients from other cultures do not understand me or are confused by what I say or do.

4. I do not fear making a sales call on persons from minority groups any more than I fear calling on persons from the dominant culture.

5. Persons from other cultures have a right to be angry at members of my culture.

6. Persons from other cultures who don't actively participate during a sales call may act that way because of their culture's rules.

7. How I handle objections with persons from other cultures depends on the situation and the cultures they are from.

8. My culture is not superior to others.

9. I am knowledgeable of how to behave with persons of different cultures.

10. I respect the communication rules of cultures other than my own.

The more statements you label as true, the more prepared you are to enter the global sales arena.

Culture impacts selling. Every day, sales professionals find themselves facing situations in which they need to interact with, communicate competently with, and influence persons culturally different from themselves. Not all succeed.

Controlling the Cost of Cultural Ignorance

Even the most experienced sales representatives can find a sale blocked because of the rep's unfamiliarity with the cultural arena or context. Because of lack of knowledge, targets the salesperson wants as clients may perceive the agent as insensitive, ignorant, or culturally confused. Cultural confusion exacts a high price from the bottom line of sales professionals. The following examples demonstrate just how costly cultural ignorance can be:

• Showing the sole of a shoe means nothing to observers in the United States or Europe. As a result, when calling on a Saudi client, American and European reps might think nothing about crossing their legs and pointing their shoes toward their target while listening to him explain his concerns. The client, however, could be horrified. In Muslim cultures, the gesture is perceived as insulting. Similarly, while crossing your legs when with a client in the United States indicates you are relaxed, in Korea it is a social faux pas.

• John, a sales executive with an American multinational corporation, had difficulty establishing a relationship with his Taiwanese customer. As John's nervousness increased, his eye-blink rate increased. This only made things worse. Taiwanese consider blinking while another person talks impolite.

• Japanese business people view the business card as the extension of a person; in contrast, Americans see it as a business formality and convenience. Thus, an American sales rep is often too quick to put a Japanese client's card away and as a result may unwittingly insult the customer.

• American sales reps place a high value on eye-to-eye communication and are likely to distrust persons who fail to make eye contact. Arabs are similarly apt to maintain direct contact with those they interact with for prolonged periods. In contrast, the Japanese believe that sustained eye contact conveys disrespect. Persons from Asian cultures tend to find extended eye contact intrusive.

• When an American sells to an American they benefit from stressing personal achievement and individualism. When selling to persons of Asian or Native American cultures, they might do better to stress how the product or service offered will promote group cohesion and loyalty, placing more emphasis on group rather than individual incentives.

In this age of increased cultural contact, enhancing cultural competence is essential.

Using Culture to Guide Sales Scripts

Ethnocentrism, the tendency to see one's own culture as superior to all others, is a key reason sales efforts fail. Ethnocentric sales reps lack cultural flexibility and are particularly unprepared to meet the sales challenges posed by selling across cultures. By interpreting the behavior of customers solely on the basis of their own frame of reference, instead of creating new opportunities for understanding, ethnocentric sales reps create openings for misunderstandings.

Culture is the lens through which sales reps and clients need to view the world. Among the lessons culture teaches are how to begin and terminate a sales call, when to speak or remain silent, how to act when pleased or disappointed, where to focus your eyes when speaking or listening, how much to gesture, and how close to stand to a client.

Becoming familiar with cultural dialectics—*task versus relationship, individualism versus collectivism, high context versus low context, high power distance versus low power distance*, and *masculine versus feminine* culture—can provide guidance as well as help turn prospects from cultures different from yours into loyal customers. Not turning customers off starts with reducing the strangeness of strangers.

Task Versus Relationship: How Much "Zig-Zag" Time Is Desirable?

Task-focused sales reps expect to close deals quickly and in rapid succession. Their sole motivation for getting together with clients is to accomplish sales. Once a sale is made, they rapidly move on to the next prospect. Their pace is quick. From their perspective, time is money and a scarce commodity. A significant number of reps from the United States or Canada are focused in this way; they expect to get right to the point of the sales meeting and right to work. Characteristically, they also tend to put business before pleasure.

So what happens when a rep from a task-oriented country such as the Untied States has a prospect from a more relationship-oriented culture such as Mexico? For one thing, when working with relationship-oriented prospects, task-oriented reps need to be ready to extend their sales trips. Rather than getting right to work, they will likely need to spend time promoting good relations and the benefits of working together. Instead of coming directly to the point, the sales meetings they have will benefit from having more of a "zig-zag" feel. That is, they need to "zig" from relationship building and "zag" into the work itself.

Individualism Versus Collectivism: When Should You Group-Up?

The cultural dimension of individualism versus collectivism reveals how people define themselves in relationship to others. When it comes to decision making, some cultures are more individually oriented, while others are more group oriented. Individualistic cultures such as those of Great Britain, the United States, Canada, France, and Germany stress individual goals, whereas collectivistic cultures represented by many Arab, African, Asian, and Latin American countries give precedence to group goals and the reaching of a consensus. Pressuring for an individual of those cultures to make a buying decision by using a hard close could be a costly error. While the "I" may be most important in individualistic cultures, the "we" is the dominant force in collectivist ones.

When selling to persons who share an individualist orientation, use those "I" statements and refer to individual outcomes. When selling to persons from a collectivist culture, instead of placing emphasis on developing the prospect's sense of self, place it on helping the individual fit into the group. You might, for example, emphasize the family when speaking to persons from Latin American cultures, or the community when speaking to members of African cultures.

High Context Versus Low Context: It's in the Interpretation?

Cultures vary in their preference for high-context or low-context communication. Cultures with high-context communication systems are tradition bound; their cultural traditions shape both the behavior and lifestyle of members, contributing to their appearing to be overly polite and indirect in relating to others. Thus, Asians and East Indians may try to soften negative responses to a sales message. Rather than say no explicitly, they may instead ask a question. Similarly, yes may mean "I hear you," rather than "I agree."

In contrast, cultures with low-context communication systems generally encourage their members to exhibit a more direct communication style.

Business people from the United States are known for holding no-holds-barred sales meetings.

When making that first sales call, keep in mind that while members of low-context cultures are likely to find it normal to be asked questions designed to help gather background information such as where they live or went to school, persons from high-context cultures are much less likely to feel comfortable when asked such questions. Persons from high-context cultures believe that most messages can be understood without significant amounts of direct verbal interaction. The Japanese have traditionally valued silence, believing that a person of few words is thoughtful, trustworthy, and respectable. In contrast, instead of adapting to this orientation, salespersons from low-context cultures too often feel that they have to explain everything directly, which sometimes makes it difficult for the prospect to preserve a sense of harmony or to save face. Such sales reps may be judged ineffective because their prospects believe they lack skills needed to interpret contextual cues.

High Power Distance Versus Low Power Distance: Who's Equal or Unequal?

How important are power differences to your customers? While some societies perceive the parties to a social interaction as equals, others see them as unequal. Individuals from high power distance cultures such as Saudi Arabia, India, and Malaysia, view power as a fact of life and are likely to make use of its referent nature. In such cultures, subordinates are usually quick to defer to superiors. When interacting with decision makers from cultures with large power distances, you should use formal titles unless asked not to. Acting overly familiar could alienate your buyer. In contrast, customers from low power distance cultures such as Sweden, Israel, and the United States, place more value on expert power. In such cultures, subordinates are known to contradict their bosses.

Masculine Versus Feminine Culture: How Do You Speak to Values?

Cultures also differ in their attitudes toward gender roles. People from Japan, Italy, Germany, Mexico, and Great Britain have been socialized to try to be dominant and competitive; they value male aggressiveness, strength, and building wealth, including the gathering of material symbols of success. They are likely to respond to financial approaches and also eager to confront conflicts head on. People from Sweden, Norway, the Netherlands, Thailand, and Chile have what is considered more feminine values. They value relationships, tenderness, and a high quality of life. They are more apt to compromise and negotiate to resolve disagreements.

It's All Sales Communication

Communication—the glue that cements sales relationships—can come undone by carelessness including using idioms that do not translate well, words with multiple meanings, or inappropriate nonverbal cues.

You May Be Using the Same Words but Are You Speaking the Same Language?

You know what you mean by the words you are using, but the meaning for the customer will be clear only if it's known. It is extremely easy for people from different cultures to misunderstand one another. Would your customer understand you if you referred to your product as the Bentley of the industry? What if you told them that they were comparing "apples and oranges" or tried to soften the blow of a product's price by noting that you would be there to soften the "damage" or "run interference?"

Nonverbal Burble

Eye contact doesn't send the same message in every culture. In the United States, for example, we believe making eye contact demonstrates respect. In Asia, however, it may mean that the receiver does not understand you or is revealing disrespect for you.

Some decision makers respond positively when a sales rep's voice rises, recognizing how the sales rep is using volume to provide emphasis and an emotional quality to the sales pitch that would be missing without it. Decision makers from Asian cultures, however, could well be confused or offended by salespeople who speak loudly or become emotional because they believe that such behavior is inappropriate. People from Asian cultures also believe that interruptions are rude. In contrast, people from European or Middle Eastern cultures are quite comfortable being interrupted and find it normal for a number of people to speak at the same time.

By mirroring (not mimicking) the behavior of the sales target, you can adapt your sales presentation to the pattern preferred by the buyer.

Stereotypes and Sales

The United States is the most demographically diverse country in the world. Approximately 32 million people (or about 12 percent) of the total U.S. population were born in another country. Because of our tendency to handle unfamiliarity and uncertainty by placing individuals we don't know well into distinct groups or categories, the stereotypes we hold may sabotage sales calls.

Stereotypes are the mental images or pictures we carry around in our heads; they function as positive or negative shortcuts to perception and guide our reactions to others. For example, racial profiling, a generalization applied to all members of a group regardless of individual differences, is just one way that stereotyping can adversely affect sales professionals. For too many, stereotypes function as conclusions rather than starting points of understanding. They will often mislead you into making false assumptions. For example, East Indians raised in the United States and attending U.S. colleges are more likely to embrace U.S. culture and make their buying decisions differently from East Indians who never left India and remain steadfast in their dedication to their home culture. The same holds true for members of other cultural groups. Making assumptions based on a prospect's heritage is dangerous.

Like stereotyping, *prejudice* describes how we feel about a group of people whom, more likely than not, we do not personally know. A negative or positive prejudgment, prejudice arises either because we want to feel more positively about the group to which we belong or because we feel others present a threat to us, real or imaginary. Because of the negative expectations that stereotypes and prejudices produce, we usually fail to make sales calls on targets that are the objects of our prejudices.

Stereotyping and prejudice reduce tolerance for ambiguity, making sales reps that rely on stereotypes or who harbor prejudices less successful in dealing with prospects from different cultures. To combat this intolerance, sales professionals need to take the following three steps:

1. Refrain from formulating expectations based solely on your own culture.

2. Refuse to isolate selling experiences to members of your own culture.

3. Eliminate any personal biases and prejudices developed over the years by making a commitment to develop sales skills and abilities appropriate to life in a multicultural world.

Age Matters

Today, more people are over the age of 65 than are under the age of 18. Like attitudes towards culture, attitudes towards age also affect the selling process. Sales professionals can benefit from understanding how to sell to clients both older and younger than themselves.

In general, potential customers who are older tend to be less receptive to having strangers call them. For this reason, you will need to establish your credibility rather quickly. You also need to be respectful without giving into the ageism that could lead them to perceive you as patronizing.

Keep in mind that people who have distance between their ages have lived through different historical periods and may be operating with different assumptions and experiences. Age influences both behavior and the expectations of others. How we categorize someone, for example, as a member of a youth or senior citizen subculture, affects how we interact with that person. We might meet an older woman and assume based on her grandmotherly appearance that she is nurturing, sheltering, and gentle. (There we go stereotyping again!) Similarly, we might categorize a young person as aggressive, self-obsessed, and rude based merely on the clothing that she or he is wearing. Because we carry our sense of age identity from sales encounter to sales encounter, ageism may contribute to the feeling that we know more than they do.

In countries that emphasize status differences, age is a benefit, as these proverbs about youth reveal:

The eggshell is still on your butt. (Hungarian)

There is blood on your head and it is not dried off yet. (Korean)

He who has no hair on his lip can't be trusted to do anything well. (Chinese)

Youth is an illness that time cures. (Spanish)

When it comes to persons from different cultures, the older the person, the more likely they are to adhere to the traditional beliefs of their native culture.

Age prejudice, whether directed at the young or more aged, contributes to sales people acting on mistaken assumptions. In fact when it comes to aging, our society's worshipping of youth and deep-seated fear of growing older promotes the use of negative stereotypes that reveal themselves in jokes and conversation. Aging in the United States appears to correlate with decrease perceived value. Don't fall into this trap. Sales reps also need to recognize that some older clients are more skeptical and cautious than younger people. They may take more time during conversations, requiring you to provide them with information that assures them of the wisdom of a purchase. And unlike many younger people, they are more comfortable saying, "I don't know."

Do you feel equally adept at selling across age groups?

Gender Matters

Using inclusive language can facilitate selling. Altering your sales presentation to reflect how men and women, in general, prefer to be perceived and treated enables you to practice adaptive selling. For example, from the salesperson's perspective, not stereotyping women as weak and emotional and men as strong and rational is a prerequisite for sales success. From the client's perspective, female sales reps who use assertive speech patterns associated with masculinity are likely to be perceived as arrogant or rude, while male sales reps who use emotional language associated with femininity are apt to be seen as wimpy.

Because of the way they have been socialized, men are likely to respond to sales presentations that are direct and assertive, seek to solve problems, or enhance their status. They like to be able to assert their ideas and voice their opinions. Men also offer minimal response cues. Women, in contrast, are likely to respond to salespeople that create relationships with them through talk, include them in their presentations, probe gently to develop a fuller understanding of them, and don't criticize them but are emotionally responsive towards them. Because they also tend to be more risk aversive than men, it is wise to provide women with sufficient information to reduce ambiguous feelings about making a purchase.

Do you feel equally adept at selling to men and women?

Wearing Down the Culture Barrier

Being able to attune yourself to the culture of your clients will help you be more effective in selling across cultures. Sales borders exist in your mind only. In reality, the world of selling is borderless!

Technology, MEdia, and Sales

In addition to recognizing culture's influence on sales, equally critical for sales reps of the 21st century is the understanding of how to use technological innovations as sales tools. Like any tool, technology when used appropriately can pave the salesperson's way, augment face-to-face selling, and facilitate follow-up.

Face Up to the MEdia Revolution

We are convinced that the word *media* should now be spelled *MEdia*. Why? Because *Generation Me*, that cohort born after 1970, is the generation that's now leading the charge into the future. This generation expects others to be as thrilled with them as they are with themselves. Members of Generation Me grew up using computers as their primary means of interaction. They are also natural media multitaskers. They chat on cellphones, surf the Internet, IM or TM (instant message or text message), read e-mail on their BlackBerries, and listen to podcasts, all while planning their day's appointments. Generation Me's members are used to focusing on themselves, and they want you to focus on them. They need their daily dose of what media expert Nicolas Negroponte calls "The Daily Me."

Generation Me members also use an array of technological tools to help them express themselves, develop online communities, and personalize their media environments and schedules. If you're selling to members of this cohort, or if you are a member of this cohort yourself, keep in mind that Generation Me members have huge goals, a yearning for self-fulfillment, pride themselves on their individualism, but may be somewhat sketchy when it comes to execution. The key to reaching Gen Me: They want my media or I media, not mass media. Thus, you need to appeal to their individuality and help them feel good about themselves because they often place themselves at the head of their priority list. Your task is to turn them from passive receiver or consumer of sales information into active creator of sales content. They feel entitled to be in the spotlight and the subject of your attention. When you're as plugged into iPods, cell phones, and laptops as Gen Me members are, when you love *MySpace* and *YouTube* and can escape to *Second Life*, it just gets easier to shut out the rest of the world, doesn't it? It's your job to break through and make them happy by soliciting their input and handing them back control. They want their access to information to be immediate. They want their access to you "always on."

E-Mail: Break Through

If you haven't used e-mail as a sales tool, now is the time to begin! If you are already using it, there's always room for improvement. But first a caution: E-mail is not a replacement for the phone or face-to-face contact. It needs to be perceived as a sales supplement that can add to the power of a sales call or even create one.

If you find yourself repeatedly blocked by the gatekeeper, e-mail can help you break through the barrier. Most often, however, it is not a way to create new relationships, but a backup option for more personal contact. Thus, e-mail is particularly useful in establishing continuing relationships with customers and preventing customer defections. By using e-mail to maintain regular contact and keep clients "warm," you decrease the chances of their perceiving you as indifferent to them or their needs.

In addition to enabling you to literally be omnipresent by keeping you front and center in the minds of clients, e-mail also lets you communicate with unlimited numbers of existing and potential customers, provides an easy way for you to remind prospects and customers of the benefits that your product or service offers, and serves as an effective means of priming your call for action.

Here are some guidelines to keep in mind when using e-mail:

• Write a compelling subject line that concisely summarizes the e-mail's central idea or purpose. Keep your company name out of it. Your goal is to create a "must open" mind-set in receivers. Making the subject line talk by including a verb and referencing a problem you may be able to help customers solve increases the likelihood they open and read it.

• Begin with a friendly salutation and be yourself. Introduce yourself and your company in the first paragraph. The primary purpose of e-mailing is to make friends or sustain a friendship. Prospects and customers respond to friends; like you, they remember the old adage about not talking to strangers. Become the un-stranger.

• Frontload your e-mail. By revealing the main idea immediately and directly, you amplify the e-mail's purpose. Busy receivers want to know immediately why they're reading your message.

• Write a brief, pressure-free message that is understandable and gets to the point. Most e-mail recipients do not read the messages they receive in their entirety. Instead, they read the first few sentences and make a decision about whether to continue reading. Your message should make them want to continue. Don't fill the message with abbreviations others might have difficulty understanding. Write out words and phrases. Even FYI or ASAP can be misinterpreted.

• The goal of your e-mail is to spark future phone or face-to-face dialogue. An e-mail message should not be a sales pitch. Instead it should be clear, concise, and contain information or documents your customers need.

• Write flawless messages. The e-mails you send reflect you and either raise or lower your credibility. Show you care. Proofread. Fix run-on sentences, sentence fragments, sloppy punctuation, and typos. Use simple, direct, under-standable language. Use readable fonts—not a mix of different ones.

• To keep your message easy on the eye, break up the text with line breaks and white space. Use headings and bullets to make it easy to scan. Also, don't use all capital letters to make a point. What all caps suggest to others is that the sender is angry. That's not the message you want to send. Keep the tone friendly.

• Provide flawless service. Give all the information a prospect or cus-tomers need to contact you or buy from you should they desire to do so. Have a single call to action—the one thing you want the receiver to do—click to open and view a catalog or express interest in your product or service.

• Sign off positively.

Blogs: Reach Out

Posting information of concern to prospects or customers can be beneficial to sales. A blog (short for weblog) is an interactive online journal, casually written, that can help you share information, promote products, and re-spond to customer concerns. And since visitors to a blog typically leave pub-lic comments, it can also make you more approachable as well as provide you with special insight into your clients.

You can use a blog to discuss new products, show customers how to use new features of an existing product, or answer customer questions. If you give your blog "a great idea just occurred to me" tone, the thinking is it might well become addictive. Reaching out by providing interesting reports on or opinions about products and services, or interviews and articles re-lated to your product or service gives the reader of your blog something they want. You also need to be sure to ask for reader comments or opinions. Ask readers to describe their experiences or ask them to suggest something. Show them you're open to their suggestions.

To be a good blogger, you need to keep a few things in mind:

• Write about what you think will interest others. You need to keep the reader in mind. If there's nothing in it for them, they won't come back.

- Write like you speak and share your personal experiences and opinions.

- Keep all posts short and simple, jazzy, and snazzy. Spoon-feed rather than misfeed readers.

- Solicit reader input.

Before making a post, take the time you need to answer each of the following questions with a "yes":

- Does the post have a headline that clarifies your topic?

- Does the lead paragraph of your post reveal who and what the post is about as well as why the reader should care?

- Is the angle you've adopted likely to interest readers?

- Is your writing jargon-free?

- Did you end with a question designed to evoke reader comments?

If you follow the guidelines provided, answer each of the preceding questions affirmatively, always keep your readers in mind, and let your personality and values come through, your blog will bring you closer to your customers. Remember, when blogging, it is important to post regularly, focus on communication, and keep every message clear and concise.

Language Success Secrets

What Is Success?

If the scripts in this manual are to help you succeed, you need to take a moment to determine what success means to you. How do you know when you have attained success and are successful? When you achieve the success you desire, is it enough to sustain you forever, or do you keep on reaching, growing, climbing? Take a minute right now to reflect on these sentence starters:

For me, success is symbolized by . . .
I will believe I am successful when I . . .
Once I accomplish that, I will be able to . . .

Salespeople define success in different ways. For some, it means a Maserati, a Jacuzzi, designer clothes, or a trip to the Super Bowl. For others it's a housekeeper, a new home, or a six-figure income. And for still others, it is a vacation the whole family can enjoy without worrying about what has to be sacrificed to pay for it. Whatever success means to you, it is important that you picture it clearly, imprint it in your memory, and carry it wherever you go. For that's the fuel you're going to need to get better—the fuel you're going to use to sell like magic!

Success does not come easy; you know that. If you settle for less than you are capable of, it might seem easy, but then you're selling yourself short. And that's never what you want to do. Other people may treat you unfairly from time to time. That's unfortunate. When you treat yourself unfairly, however, it is far worse. And that's what happens when you don't develop the confidence you need to believe in your own abilities and the skills you need to deliver yourself from mediocrity.

How many answers can you list for the following sentence starter?

A successful salesperson is ...

_____

_____

_____

How many of your answers are descriptive of a salesperson's attitude? How many responses are descriptive of his or her skill? What attributes do you need to develop or improve?

Success depends on motivation and skill for its longevity. Salespeople who experience short-lived successes usually suffer from motivational malnutrition, attitude dystrophy, or knowledge apathy. Let's explore each and determine if you possess or have experienced any symptoms.

Motivational Malnutrition.   A steady diet of motivation from both internal and external sources is necessary for a salesperson's survival. Were it not for motivation, sales plans would neither be made nor carried out. Business development strategies would cease, and selling efforts would shrink away.

Assess your personal motivation level by answering yes or no to these questions:

1. Do you greet each day feeling you will accomplish something?
   ___ Yes ___ No

2. Do you look forward to calling a stranger who might become a prospect?

___ Yes ___ No

3. Do you receive encouragement from your family and your boss on a regular basis?

___ Yes ___ No

4. Do you always find yourself happy about being in the sales profession?

___ Yes ___ No

5. Do you give yourself a pep talk after a disappointment, and try again?

___ Yes ___ No

6. Do you believe that if you keep at it, eventually you will get what you want?

___ Yes ___ No

If you have more no answers than yes answers, consider these principles of sales success:

- Become a professional generator of excitement.

- Extinguish your fears, and courage appears.

- Leap before you look.

- Make sales happen by making *you* happen.

Also keep in mind that as a professional salesperson, your job is to always have:

PEP

Positive Enthusiastic Persistence

Attitudinal Dystrophy.   We all enter sales with a strong belief in our own ability to make things happen, and we are convinced that we will do just that. But if care is not taken to nourish and nurture that feeling, we develop a quite different perspective and end up convinced that selling devours those who attempt to conquer it.

Consider these suggestions to overcome attitudinal dystrophy:

- Maintain your belief in the importance of sales.

- Remember that you are a professional persuader.

- All corporations live and die through sales.

- Sales is a continuing entrepreneurial challenge.

Knowledge Apathy.   Salespeople enter the field knowing nothing about selling. Their thirst for knowledge is high. Along the way something happens. From knowing nothing, they progress to knowing it all. This perception is deadly. First, it maims. Then it debilitates. Finally, it kills. Why? Because the only thing worth gaining every day is new knowledge—new ways of thinking, new ways of packaging what you know, new ways of influencing others, and new ways of developing. It is simple:

Give Up Knowing and You Give Up Growing

No salesperson knows all there is to know. Every salesperson has to learn from experience, from him- or herself, or from someone else every single day in the business.

Creating Change to Achieve Success

Making things happen is what the proficient salesperson does. Making things happen is your job. When you make enough things happen right, a smile is on everyone's face. A lack of smiles calls for change. But what can you change to help yourself make things happen right and to make yourself more successful at what you do than you are right now?

- You can change your environment.

- You can change the people you work with.

- You can change yourself.

Changing your environment is possible, but not totally within your control. Some environments are more conducive to success than others. It is as if they were planned to promote success and breed production. But we know that high producers work equally well in gorgeous settings as in lackluster surroundings. So something else must also be at play. The environment is the icing, not the cake.

Changing the people you work with is also possible, but again not totally up to you. We all work better with certain types of people than with others. But we do not live in vacuums where we control who enters our career bubble and who is barred at the door. We cannot pick buyers the way we pick fruit at the store. If you are to achieve real success, you need to be flexible, versatile, and open to possibilities.

Changing yourself, then, is the key to becoming more successful, and it is the one thing within your control that will influence the way you think about you, the way you act toward others, the way you communicate, and the results you achieve.

Changing is not easy. Try this:

1. Fold your hands the way you normally do. Notice which thumb you place on top.

2. Unfold your hands.

3. Fold them again, but this time, fold them so the opposite thumb ends up on top.

4. Unfold them and fold them again.

Did you fold them the new way or the old way? If you are like most people who try this exercise in our seminars, you folded them the old comfortable way, the way you are used to. Why? Because old habits die hard and new habits need time to replace them. Here are two things you can change immediately: your outlook and your demeanor.

Optimism! Yes!

Some of us consider ourselves optimists. If we suffer a defeat, we view it as a temporary setback brought about by circumstances, bad luck, or other people. Salespeople who are optimists are resilient; they do not view defeat as their own fault. Other people categorize themselves as pessimists. In contrast to optimists, pessimists lack resilience and believe that bad events are their own fault, will last a long time, and will undermine whatever they do in sales. Instead of believing they can control their own destiny, they believed that outside forces determine their fate.

In one study, swimmers were told that their times were slower than they actually were. The optimists responded by swimming the next heat faster, while swimmers who considered themselves pessimists swam the next heat slower. Thus you can see that it is important to be an optimist, that is, to establish what many people call a positive attitude. Trainer Jeffrey Gitomer calls it the "Yes!" attitude. We score a touchdown, hit a home run, score a goal and scream "Yes!" We need to do the same thing everytime we make a sale! Yes!!

Let's Be Nice!

As kids we are told to be nice. "Be nice to the dogs!" "Be nice to your Aunt!" Somehow when we get into business, we sometimes forget these admonitions. We might be nice to the president, but what about the doormen, assistants, cabbies, and waiters?

Think of someone you know who is nice to you. Now think of someone who is not nice to you. Which person would you be more apt to refer business to? Recommend for a job? Approve a loan? Of course, the person who is nice. In their wonderful book, *The Power of Nice*, Linda Kaplan Thaler and Robin Koval suggest that we listen, admire, and praise others—consistently. We knew a fine salesperson and entrepreneur who did just that. He called everyone by name. Always knew what their spouses and kids were doing. He was the epitome of nice. We learned that this entrepreneur had learned to be nice. He came into sales from the law enforcement business where his job was to be anything but nice. He made it his business to change his approach to others.

Using Powertalk Successfully

Effective salespeople around the world are powertalkers. In contrast to those who announce their powerlessness through their speech, powertalkers communicate a sense of control and confidence and thus help to direct the buying action.

Besides being in full command of the words they use, powertalkers also use fewer hesitations, fewer tentative phrases or qualifiers, and fewer unnecessary intensifiers. Thus, powertalkers make definite statements like "Let's write up the order," rather than weaker hedges like "I think we should write up the order." Powertalkers evoke more confidence and enhance perceptions of their self-worth by not making statements filled with hesitations like "I wish you would, uh, give me an idea, um, of what you're looking for, er, in a product." In like fashion, by eliminating powerless words from their message, powertalkers actually strengthen the position they take. Hence powertalkers say, "I'm not interested in debating the issue" rather than use the weaker and more submissive, "I'm not very interested in debating the issue." Powertalkers have mastered the art of coming directly to the point. Their speech does not contain disclaimers like "I probably shouldn't mention this, but. . . ."

Powertalkers are not confrontational. They are persuasive. They ask lots of questions that offer options, such as "Would you like to meet in the morning or would you prefer the afternoon," or "Would you like delivery on Monday or Friday?"

Our female readers should take note that, interestingly, in our culture, women tend to use more tentative phrases or qualifiers in their speech than men do. Such phrases as "I guess," "I think," and "I wonder if" commonly turn up in the speech patterns of women but not in those of men. Similarly, women tend to turn statements into questions more often than men do. Women typically ask something like "Don't you think it would be better to try our product before reordering from our competitor?" In contrast, men typically come across with a more definitive statement, such as, "Try our product before reordering from our competitor."

Powertalk is talk that increases your credibility and your ability to influence others. It makes sense to use it. Changing the power balance in selling may be as simple as changing the words you use!

Sales Nonverbal Investigators

We also suggest that you work to become a Sales Nonverbal Investigator (SNVI). We know that the messages that clients send us are 60 to 90 percent nonverbal; that is, most of what people say is expressed in other ways than words. Nonverbal communication is worthy of a book on its own, so we provide just some highlights here.

Customers broadcast their emotions through their faces. Therefore, it is important for the effective sales professional to watch (investigate) what is happening in the client's face. Watching eye movements and facial expressions will help you make sales.

Research suggests that we should watch the movement in the customer's eyes for clues to what he or she is thinking.

- If the person looks up, he or she may be recalling something seen in the past, such as the product, the color, size or shape of a design, and so on.

- If the person looks to right or left, he or she may be recalling something heard, such as what the boss told him to do or what the spouse told her to pick up on the way home.

- If the person looks down, he or she may be experiencing emotion. Trying to make a buying decision might be accompanied by a downward gaze.

When talking to clients face-to-face, be sure to watch the eye movements. Try to determine how these movements relate to the information being expressed verbally.

To watch the client's facial expressions, mentally divide the face into two segments:

- The upper face: above the eyes

- The lower face: from the eyes to the bottom of the chin

Work in front of a mirror or with a partner and try on the following emotions. Note the clues in both parts of the face.

Surprise

    Upper face: Brows curved and high

    Lower face: Eyes wide open; jaw drops

Happiness

    Upper face: Remains calm

    Lower Face: Lip corners up; mouth may part; wrinkles to sides of eyes

Anger

    Upper Face: Eyebrows drawn together; vertical lines between brows

    Lower face: Lips pressed together

Disgust

    Upper face: Remains calm

    Lower face: Nose wrinkled; corner of mouth raised (as if something smells bad)

Sadness

    Upper face: Inner corners of brows raised

    Lower face: Corner of lips down

The best way to practice nonverbal investigations is to work with still photos. Examine faces in magazines, newspapers, and on the web. Use a form like the one shown here to make notes for analysis.

Nonverbal Investigation Form

1. Eye Movement:
   Looking up?
   Looking side to side?
   Looking down?

2. Facial Expression
   Upper face
   Lower face

Conclusions about the emotions displayed in the photograph: _____
_____

Of course, nonverbal investigations can be a lifelong study. What we have covered here is enough to get you started. Remember to conduct the investigation when working with your clients!

Our attitude, our ability to be nice to everyone around us, the way we communicate, and the way we read our prospects and customers can all be enhanced and changed. Change requires dedicated, conscious effort on your part. To be sure, many of the words and phrases you find in the scripts in this book will be uncomfortable at first, but once they become part of your powertalk, they will serve you and your company well. So, open the window and let some new words, actions, and attitudes inside! Let's get started. We know you will increase sales—almost like magic.

··· **ACT II** ···

ACTION!

When Using Sensible Selling

The tide is going out. The shore is littered with empty shells and one or two beached whales. Where are you? Riding the wave of the future, or stuck in the sand? If you are stuck in the sand, it is time to take action to get unstuck. If, however, you are riding the wave of the future, then you are actively working to increase your share of sales. You're actively working to find those prospects who can use what it is you have to sell. You're actively working to locate prospects to whom you can tell your exciting sales story. You are actively working to stay afloat. Where does your buoyancy come from? It comes from people.

In sales, people are your business. If you're stuck in the sand, you can't go out and find people; you have to hope they come and find you. And, as you know all too well, that's not the way things work. Rescues are a rarity. Only if you're willing to ride the wave and take the risk of being rejected do you truly stand a chance of having some extraordinary things begin to happen to you during your sales career.

To succeed, you must be able to create demand in decision makers. You need to put yourself in the position to create sales opportunities, not merely in position to respond to them. It's time to get on the phone or get in your car. It's time to find, talk to, see, and sell to people. After all, before you can sell something to someone, you have to have someone to sell to. Makes sense, doesn't it? We call it "sensible selling"—and it works. Here's why and how.

If You Don't Have a Prospect, There's No Sale to Close.

Why Sensible Selling Works

Finding a first job in sales isn't terribly difficult, is it? Rumor has it that if you pass the "living, breathing, moving, talking, driving test," you can have your choice of companies to work for. Thus, you are a marketable commodity. Many sales managers are willing to take a chance on you. They either train you formally, or they train you informally by allowing you to learn (not necessarily earn) by making expensive mistakes. Getting hired as a sales rep by a company is not usually a taxing problem; however, being certain that at the time you're hired by a company, you also remember to "hire yourself" is.

What does it mean to hire yourself? Picture this. It's Monday morning. You arrive at the office for a regional sales meeting. Other reps are milling around talking about how productive or frustrating their territories are. The sales manager calls the meeting to order. New reps are introduced. Those who landed new clients or made big sales are recognized for their superior performances. All are urged to increase their efforts and produce more. Tips and encouragement are passed out freely, as are sales rep excuses. It's the excuses you have to watch out for. Why? Because sensible selling is "no-excuse selling."

Excuse Selling

Next time you are in the company of a group of sales representatives, list, but don't take to heart, the excuses they offer to explain why they haven't closed enough business this year. After identifying the excuses they use—of course, you never use those excuses, do you?—indicate how the negative excuse could be turned into a positive plan for action.

"Excuse selling" provides salespeople with just what the meaning of the words suggests. "To excuse" means "to make apology for" and "to try to remove blame from." A salesperson who offers excuses for inactivity or a lack of production is trying to hold himself or herself blameless for the lack of results. Instead, the finger of blame points away from the salesperson and is aimed at—well, you name it:

- Market conditions
- The sales manager
- The dealer
- The client
- The advertising
- Lack of support
- The weather

That is, anything and everything but the salesperson is to blame. In fact, excuses commonly begin with, "I'm trying as hard as I can but. . . ." Although most people say they are trying, in truth they are not.

So what do salespeople who are stuck in the sand have to teach you? The answer is "the art of excusing." And what does the art of excusing lead to? The answer is *"losing."*

Help Enough of Your Prospects
Get What They Want, and You'll
Get What You Want, Too!

So, wipe excuse selling from your slate of appropriate strategies and in its place substitute doing what produces results. For the truth is that excusing yourself for a lack of results may make you feel better in the short term, but it won't turn you into an effective sales machine. It won't turn you into salesperson of the year. Riding the sales wave and doing what advances your career will. For this reason, let's equate hiring yourself with no-excuse selling, and let's equate no-excuse selling with running your own career advancement program (CAP).

You Hire YOU!

You see, when you hire your YOU, you take responsibility for your performance. You chart your progress and you monitor your results. When you hire YOU, you give up waiting, you give up complaining, you give up passivity. When you hire YOU, you increase your chances of succeeding beyond your wildest dreams. You no longer sit back and watch. YOU jump in and do!

> *Prospects Need to Believe*
> *They'll Be Better Off if They Buy from*
> *YOU!*

Now that you know the why, it is time to look at the how.

How Sensible Selling Works

First, consider all your work time as business development time. This perspective will prevent you from thinking of yourself as a passive recipient of business and will cause you instead to see yourself as an active creator of business.

Second, think of business development time as prime time. Consider every business development minute as true opportunity time. Use the time to develop leads, follow up on inquiries, build rapport with potential customers and referrals, and establish your credibility as a source with the people whose business you desire.

Third, keep yourself on track. Track your daily business development results on a form like the one provided here. Examine your results to determine if your prospecting time is well spent and productive. Usually, it takes at least ten prospecting calls to get a single appointment with a decision maker. How many calls does it take you? If you are making lots of calls and landing few, if any, appointments with decision makers, you may be turning prospects off rather than on to you and your product or service. The scripts that follow will help you prospect more efficiently, enabling you to double, triple or quadruple the sales call appointments you actually make. More appointments will help you increase your sales, and increasing your sales increases your income. You can do it! You can ride the wave to success.

Daily Business Development

Date: _____

Time: from _____ to _____

Number of cold calls made to solicit new business: _____

Number of cold calls made in response to inquiries: _____

Number of cold calls made as a result of referrals: _____

Number of calls made to existing accounts: _____

Number of calls made to previous accounts: _____

Number of *appointments* scheduled as a result of the above: _____

If calling residences, be sure to check Do Not Call lists.

Cold Calls to New Customers

(Of course, if you are calling residences, you will follow your company guidelines to stay in compliance with the Do Not Call regulations.)

 ### *The "Basic" Script*

Hello, [*Mr./Ms. Prospect*].

This is [*your name*] from [*your company*].

I'm calling to introduce you to our [*your product/service*].

If there were a way I could help you meet your goals or objectives or even surpass them, you'd want to hear about it, wouldn't you?

> *Pause two seconds, but do not expect a verbal answer.*

What I'd like to do, [*Mr./Ms. Prospect*], is talk about that with you in person. Can we meet on [*day*], or would [*another day*] be better? Would [*time*] in the morning be good, or is another time in the afternoon better? I'm looking forward to meeting you.

The "Better Way" Script

Hello, [*Mr./Ms. Prospect*].

This is [*your name*] from [*your company*].

Say excitedly:

I'm calling to offer you a better way of doing business. When we meet I'll show you how our [*your product/service*] will get you the results you'd like to see. Now, can we meet on [*day*], or would [*another day*] be better?

The "Sold to Another" Script

This statement carries a risk with it. Be aware that many companies want exclusive supply or limited distribution.

Hello, [*Mr./Ms. Prospect*].

This is [*your name*] from [*your company*]. I'd like you to know that last week I sold [*your product/service*] to [*another company*]. Since both [*the other company*] and you are in the same business, I thought you might want to have the *same* competitive advantage they have. Having that same advantage is important to you, isn't it?

I'm available to meet with you on [*day*] at [*time*], or would [*another day*] at [*another time*] be better?

The "What Do You Look For?" Script

Hello, [*Mr./Ms. Prospect*].

This is [*your name*] from [*your company*]. Do you have a minute to talk?

A positive response or silence gives you permission to continue.

[*Mr./Ms. Prospect*], have you considered that you could benefit from using [*your product/service*]? What do you look for in a [*your product/service*]? If I can show you that our [*your product/service*] meets or surpasses those requirements, that would interest you, wouldn't it?

Always close for the appointment when you can.

Would you like to meet with me on [*day*] at [*time*], or would [*another day*] at [*another time*] be better?

The "Add to Your Business" Script

Hello, [*Mr./Ms. Prospect*].

This is [*your name*] from [*your company*]. Have you ever thought about how you could add to the business you've built by using [*your product/service*]? I'd like to show you just that.

Can we get together on [*day*] at [*time*], or would [*another day/time*] be better?

The "Leader" Script

Hello, [*Mr./Ms. Prospect*].

This is [*your name*] from [*your company*]. How are you today?

My company is regarded as a leader in [*your product/service*], and I thought you'd be interested in learning how our [*your product/service*] can enhance the leadership image your company has as well.

Say with a sense of authority:

Being perceived as a leader in your field is important to you, [*Mr./Ms. Prospect*], isn't it?

The next few scripts require you to insert a dollar figure [*$x*] that your product or service will save the buyer or user.

 ### The "Important Facts" Script

Hello, [*Mr./Ms. Prospect*].

I'm [*your name*] from [*your company*].

I have some important facts to share with you.

   Go right on.

My company's [*product/service*] will save you [*$x*] a year. I'd like to show you how. [*Mr./Ms. Prospect*], you *are* interested in saving [*$x*] next year, aren't you? It's worth just [*number*] minutes of your time to find out how, isn't it?

The calendar indicates that a good time for us to meet is [*day*] at [*time*], or would [*another day/time*] be better?

The "Increase the Bottom Line" Script

Hello, [*Mr./Ms. Prospect*].

I'm [*your name*] from [*your company*].

In just a few minutes I can show you how you can increase your bottom line by at least [*number*] percent.

Increasing your bottom line *is* something that you'd like to do, isn't it?

The "Give You Dollars" Script

Good day, [*Mr./Ms. Prospect*].

I'm pleased to be able to give you [*$x*].

At this point, the prospect asks how you can do that, and you have the opening you need to give the rest of your presentation.

The "Make Life Easier" Script

Good day, [*Mr./Ms. Prospect*].

I'm [*your name*] from [*your company*].

It's a pleasure to be [*speaking/meeting*] with you. How important is it to you to increase your bottom line?

Few prospects will say "not very."

Good. I'd like to introduce you to our [*your product/service*]. It will help you reach your goal and make your life a whole lot easier. You *are* interested in reaching your goal?

The "Companies Like Yours" Script

Hello, [*Mr./Ms. Prospect*].

I'm [*your name*] with [*your company*].

You'll be interested to know that our [*your product/service*] is being used by [*number*] companies like yours. You'll discover that you and [*prospect's company*] can benefit from using it too.

The calendar suggests we get together on [*day*] at [*time*], or is [*another day/time*] more convenient for you?

This next script is easy to remember and makes it hard for the prospect to answer no.

 ### The "Higher Profits" Script

This is a real interest arouser.

Hello, [*Mr./Ms. Prospect*].

I'm [*your name*] with [*your company*].

Does the possibility of higher profits next year appeal to you? If we get together, I can show you a number of ways you can increase those profits.

Let's do it on [*day*] at [*time*], or is [*another day/time*] better?

The "Economy Is Impacting All Business Today" Script

Hello, this is [*your name*] with [*your company*]. Has the economy impacted your business, making it absolutely necessary to do more with less? I would like the opportunity to meet with you to demonstrate how our [*your product/service*] can help you accomplish that goal.

Calls to Referrals

The "We've Worked For" Script

Say confidently:

Hello, [*Mr./Ms. Referral*]. [*Name of referring source*] suggested I call you. We've done quite a bit of work for [*referring source*]. [*He/she*] and [*referring company*] found our work helpful and thought we might be of service to you too.

The "Client of Mine" Script

Say assuredly:

[*Mr./Ms. Referral*], my special reason for calling on you today is at the suggestion of [*your referring source*], who has been a client of mine since [*year*]. [*Your referring source*] is really happy with the [*ideas/programs*] we've implemented especially for [*him/her*].

In [*his/her*] opinion, these [*ideas/programs*] helped increase [*his/her*] company's [*profitability/production/morale*]. [*Referring source*] felt certain you'd like to consider what we have to offer too. Was [*he/she*] right?

Calls to Former Clients

The "In Charge" Script

Hello, [*Mr./Ms. Former Client*]. This is [*your name*] with [*your company*]. I am now in charge of this territory for my company. I understand that at one time you used our products. Is that correct?

Why did you change suppliers?

   Wait for response.

We have made a number of improvements in our [*your product/ service*] recently that I think would be of interest to you. When can we get together so I can share them with you?

The "Glad I Found You" Script

Hello, [*Mr./Ms. Former Client*]. I am so glad I found you in today. I know you are now using our competitor's [*product/service*]. Is that correct?

   Communicate that you are about to do the person a favor.

We have made some significant modifications in our product line that you should be aware of. I would be glad to demonstrate them to you so you are brought up-to-date on the latest technology in our industry. Can we get together this afternoon?

Effective Discussion Openers

 ### *The "Share an Idea" Script*

Work to create curiosity.

My special reason for wanting to meet with you is to share an idea that our clients tell us [*makes them more money/cuts costs/reduces turnover*].

The "Increasing" Script

Share your excitement with your prospect.

Does increasing [*profits/morale/productivity*] interest you?

The "Important to Increase" Script

How *important* is it to you to increase [*profits/morale/productivity*]?

The "Employees Motivated" Script

How important is it to you to keep your employees motivated and productive?

The "Help Save" Script

We've been helping companies like yours save time and money. Would you like to know how?

The You'll Appreciate" Script

Say confidently:

You're really going to appreciate what our [*your product/service*] can do for you.

The "Intrigue" Script

Enthusiasm is the key here.

The next fifteen minutes are going to intrigue you. You'll be astonished at the benefits our [*your product/service*] offers, and our time together will fly by. Let's begin to explore the possibilities.

The "Like to Save" Script

You like to save money, don't you? Then we need to talk as soon as possible!

The "Most People" Script

Most people in a position like yours feel that they need to have a [*your product/service*] like ours to accomplish their goals.

The "I'm Not Certain" Script

Say forthrightly:

[*Mr./Ms. Prospect*]. I'm not *certain* whether my ideas apply to your situation. But let me get your answer to a question. If your answer is yes, it's unlikely what I have to offer will apply. But if your answer is no, then it will truly be beneficial for both of us to spend some time with each other in an effort to discover how I can help.

Pause. My question is this: Are you *totally* satisfied with [*the amount of business your company is doing/the time it takes your employees to complete their assignments/the profits generated by your unit/what you are paying for* . . .]?

Getting By the Secretary

The "Prospect Would Want to Know" Script

Take command!

This is [*your name*]. May I speak with [*Mr./Ms. Prospect*]. I'm calling because I'm sure [*Mr./Ms. Prospect*] would want to know how our [*your product/service*] can benefit [*the company you're talking to*].

The "You'd Be Helping" Script

Say politely but firmly:

This is [*your name*]. May I ask your name? The [*your product/service*] we want to share has worked very well in companies like [*the company you're talking to*]. I really think you'd be helping your company if you let me demonstrate for [*Mr./Ms. Prospect*] the kinds of benefits to be derived from using it.

The calendar indicates that a good time for us to meet is [*day*] at [*time*], or would [*another day/time*] be better for you and [*Mr./Ms. Prospect*]?

The "Materials Needed" Script

Say with authority:

I'm [*your name*] with [*your company*]. Is [*Mr./Ms. Prospect*] in? I have the material [*he/she*] needs.

The "First and Last Name" Script

Be direct. Do not become unnerved.

This is [*your name*] from [*your company*]. [*First and last name of prospect*], please.

The "Company's Future" Script

A sense of urgency is key here.

I am [*your name*] with [*your company*]. This call is about your company's future. It's important that I speak to [*your prospect*]. Please put me through now.

The "Appreciate Your Interest" Script

Say with strength; be sure to communicate impatience, not anger.

This is [*your name*] with [*your company*]. Who am I speaking to?

I appreciate your interest in the reason for this call. Does your boss want you to prevent [*him/her*] from finding out about an important opportunity to increase profits? I'm certain [*he/she*] would be grateful if you'd connect us now.

The "On the Line" Script

Good morning. Would you please tell [*your prospect*] that [*your name*] from [*your company*] is on the line.

The "Special Reason" Script

Say kindly but directly:

My name is [*your name*] from [*your company*]. The special reason for my [*call/visit*] today is to meet [*your prospect*], state my business, and see if it will be beneficial for us to meet. Could we do that now?

The "Just Suppose" Script

Say inquisitively:

Just suppose I had an idea that would substantially increase your company's [*sales/profits/productivity*]. Wouldn't your boss want to know about it? Please connect us now.

The "Working on an Idea" Script

A confident air is important here.

We are working with a number of companies like yours on an idea that our clients tell us significantly [*improves profits/reduces turnover/ increases productivity*]. My experience tells me that the [*position of your prospect*] can quickly determine whether your company would want to consider the idea. Could I [*speak with/ meet with*] [*him/her*] now?

The "Has Boss Thanked You?" Script

The compliment works.

This is [*your name*] with [*your company*]. Has your boss ever thanked you for putting [*him/her*] in touch with someone? This will be such an opportunity. Please connect us now.

The "If There Were a Way?" Script

This is [*your name*] with [*your company*]. Please connect me to [*Mr./Ms. Prospect*].

The secretary will ask you to explain what your call is about and you answer:

By all means. If there were a way to [*increase profits/double produc-tivity/boost morale/reduce turnover*], [*Mr./Ms. Prospect*] would prob-ably want to know about it, don't you think?

The "Help Me Out" Script

Appeals for assistance are hard to turn down.

This is [*your name*] with [*your company*]. I'm hoping you can help me out.

How do you suggest I go about setting up an appointment with [*your prospect*]? I know I can count on you to let [*your prospect*] know how important it is that we get together. I'm relying on you to help me out.

The "Boss Will Know Me" Script

Is [*Mr./Ms. Prospect*] in? This is [*your name*] with [*your company*].

[*He/she*] will be familiar with my name.

The following scripts are responses to a variety of sample prospect statements you'll find throughout this chapter.

"I'm Too Busy to Talk to You Right Now."

Most prospects think they are too busy. Don't let that deter you.

 ### The "Invest Minutes" Script

I appreciate how important time is to you. You'll be pleased to discover that our [*your product/service*] will save you time and money. If you can invest just [*number*] minutes, I can help you save [*$x*]. That's a fair exchange, isn't it?

The "Profit Margin" Script

I understand your concern for time, but are you too busy to increase your profit margin?

The "Short Presentation" Script

Other people in your [*industry/business/field*] have told me exactly the same thing. And so I invested my time to shorten my presentation so it takes no more than [*number*] minutes of your time. Let's share those few minutes together. You'll find that your investment in those few minutes was a very wise decision.

The "Realize Value" Script

You can turn the prospect's excuse around and make it work in your favor.

It's because you're so busy that I want to see you. It's the busy [*executive/manager/businessperson*] like yourself who realizes the value of what we have to offer. Let's talk.

The "Demonstrate Profits" Script

You know, [*Mr./Ms. Prospect*], that others in your [*industry/business/field*] have answered exactly as you just did before I had the chance to sit down with them and demonstrate how our [*your product/service*] would increase their profits. I wonder if we might meet.

Don't pause here.

Would [*day*] at [*time*] be good, or is [*another day/time*] better?

The "Wise Decision" Script

You know [*Mr./Ms. Prospect*], a lot of people have said that. But once I had the opportunity to meet with them and share how our [*your product/service*] would help them, they made the wise decision to give us a try. My calendar indicates that [*day*] at [*time*] is clear. Or is [*another day/time*] better?

The "Your Best Customer" Script

Say this with a sense of astonishment:

Would you say that to one of your highly *valued* customers? If you spend just a few minutes with me, you'll discover that I can help you make as much money with our [*your product/service*] as you now make from your best customers

The ""Another Interruption" Script

Let your sense of humor show here. Humor can help you sell.

I understand. You probably think of me as just another interruption. Therefore, you'll be pleased to find out why this is not your run-of-the-mill sales call and why what I have to tell you will positively affect your company's bottom line. If you absolutely, positively can't talk right now, when can we get together?

The "Very Busy" Script

This script requires a very serious tone to match a prospect's tone.

You're very busy, and I'm very busy. Wasting your time would be wasting my time. I don't talk to people unless I'm convinced they can use what I have to offer. So the time you spend with me will be time well spent. The same things are important to us. Let me show you how I know.

The "Remind Me" Script

This script is designed to arouse prospect curiosity.

You remind me of [*another decision maker*] at [*a competitor*]. Your competition also thought [*he/she*] was too busy to talk to me. But af-ter meeting with me for [*number*] minutes, [*he/she*] was glad to have done so. Would you like to learn what [*he/she*] discovered during our brief time together?

The "Takes Longer to Read" Script

Don't use this if you're less interesting than a piece of paper!

I'd send you information in the mail, but it would take longer for you to read it than for me to explain it. And I'm so much more interesting and effective than a piece of paper. If time is really of the essence to you, let's talk face to face. That will save you time.

The "More Important Than Profits" Script

This one is simple, direct, and effective.

What could be more important than learning how to increase your profits?

The "Motivated Employees" Script

What could be more important than discovering how to make your employees more productive and motivated?

The "Eliminate Words" Script

My goal is to eliminate those words from your vocabulary. My [*your product/service*] will give you more time, not steal time from you.

The "Lack of Time" Script

This script isolates the time problem so you can deal with it effectively.

I understand. Is a lack of time your biggest problem right now?

The "Same Complaint" Script

That's the same complaint that [*a referral known to your prospect*] had at first. After investing a small amount of time with me, however, [*he/she*] was pleased to have taken that time to learn more about [*your product/service*]. I believe you'll have the same reaction. The calendar shows that next [*day*] at [*time*] is good, or would [*another day/time*] be better for you?

"You're Wasting Your Time."

The "Appreciate Thoughtfulness" Script

Thanking the prospect for showing concern is disarming.

I appreciate your thoughtfulness. I understand the value of time too. And that's why I think it's critical we get together for fifteen minutes. What I have to share with you could significantly affect your company's profit and productivity. Could you free up fifteen minutes on [*day*] or is [*another day*] better?

The "Still Friends" Script

This script reduces prospect fear of being captured by a zealous sales representative.

Why don't we agree to spend fifteen minutes together? If after investing that small amount of time, you don't believe we have anything further to share with each other, we'll end our discussion—still friends. If, however, you do believe that I just may be able to help you solve a problem you're facing, we'll continue sharing ideas.

We could schedule that fifteen-minute meeting next [*day*] at [*time*], or on [*another day*] at [*time*]. Which is better for you?

The "I'm Impressed" Script

This script simply turns the argument around.

I'm impressed that as busy as you are, you are still concerned about me. I appreciate that. My job is to save you time. Agreeing to invest just ten minutes with me could save you time and money tomorrow. That won't be a waste of my time, and it won't be a waste of your time either.

"I'm Not Interested."

 ## The "Just Those Words" Script

Say assuredly:

Many of our loyal customers began our relationship with just those words. It wasn't until I demonstrated how [*your product/service*] could help increase the bottom line that they became *really* interested. I'll share that same information with you now.

The "Company's Interests" Script

Be surprised.

How come? You *are* concerned about your company's interests, aren't you?

The "What Interests You?" Script

Use parallel structure for emphasis.

Does saving money interest you? Does improving productivity interest you? Does cutting down on problems interest you? If you answer yes to any of these, then you need to learn how we can help.

The "Doesn't Interest You" Script

How is it possible that saving money and saving time doesn't interest you? Wouldn't doing both make your business stronger?

The "Reaction" Script

Say this understandingly:

That's a reaction we all have at one time or another. We use it on stockbrokers, realtors, insurance agents, and so on. But often when we learn more about their products or services, and how they can benefit us, we change our minds and we become interested, and when the time is right, we buy.

I have a feeling that the same is true for us. Let me share how [*your product/service*] can work for you.

The "Not Today" Script

First, speak understandingly; then sound confused.

If you're not interested today, I understand. If you think you'll never be interested, then I'm confused. I thought you were in business to make money and increase profits and productivity. That is true, isn't it?

The "If I Communicated" Script

Search for feedback.

If that's so, I'm really sorry. I must have failed to get my message across. If I was effective in communicating the many ways [*your product/service*] would positively affect your operation, you would be interested. What didn't I get across?

The "Until I Demonstrate" Script

Say matter-of-factly:

I understand. Until I demonstrate for you how [*your product/service*] will help increase profits and improve performance, I wouldn't expect you to be interested. I just need fifteen minutes to explain how we can deliver results.

We could get together [*day*] at [*time*], or is [*another day*] at [*time*] better?

The "Consider Your Company" Script

May I ask you to consider your company's interests for a moment?

> *Pause.*

I believe our [*your product/service*] will help increase [*profits/morale/ productivity*]. Let's look at the evidence together.

The "Never Hear That" Script

> *Be astonished!*

We hardly ever hear that. Could you explain how you could not be interested in increasing [*profits/morale/productivity*]? I thought that was a key goal.

The "Surprises Me" Script

> *Isolate the problem.*

It surprises me to hear that because our [*your product/service*] would have [*a benefit of your product/service*]. Nonetheless, I'm sure you have a good reason for not having an interest. Will you share it with me?

The "Good Reason" Script

I'm sure you have a good reason for saying that. Please share it with me.

"Send Me Literature," or
"Send Me an E-Mail."

 ### The "Faster to Meet" Script

Communicate concern.

I wish the literature told the whole story. You'll be able to evaluate our [*your product/service*] a lot faster by meeting with me. It will take just fifteen minutes for you to judge whether our [*your product/service*] will be profitable for your firm. Shall we schedule that meeting on [*day*] or would [*another day*] be more convenient?

The "Interested or Not Interested" Script

Say authoritatively:

Whenever someone asks me to send literature or send an e-mail instead of making an appointment, I find that one of two things occur. Either the person is very interested in what I have to share and wants to know as much about it as possible, or the person is not at all interested and is asking me to send literature or an e-mail as an easy way to let me know that.

Just so I don't waste any of your time, because I tend to be real persistent, would you mind telling me which of these possibilities applies to you?

If it's the latter, say:

I'm sure you have a good reason for feeling that this isn't of interest to you. Would you please share that with me?

The "Fifteen Minutes" Script

Literature frequently raises more questions than it answers. I know your time is valuable. In just fifteen minutes I can demonstrate how our [*your product/service*] will benefit you.

The calendar shows that [*day*] at [*time*] is good for us to get together, or is [*another day*] at [*time*] better?

The "Unfair to Both" Script

Become the diplomat.

Doing that would be unfair to us both. The literature may raise key questions that I could easily answer. You'll have a much clearer picture of the kinds of benefits our [*your product/service*] delivers if we meet for just fifteen minutes. Which day is more convenient for you— [*day*] or [*another day*]?

Controlling the Sale

Sales Professionals Control Buyers, They Don't Just Visit With Them.
If You're Visiting Your Buyers, You Are Taking a Selling Vacation.

Right now, you could probably name a number of things you'd like to do differently when working with buyers. Some of these changes, if you actually followed through on them, might well mean the difference between your earning $30,000 per year and $300,000 per year! The point is that if you change the way you work with buyers, if you take steps to control the sale, you also take steps toward earning more money.

Controlling the Buyer: The Key to Your Success

As a prelude to "taking charge" of the buyer, it's important to examine those behaviors or forces that can prevent you from doing so. Some are psychological, such as your fears or insecurities, whereas others are habits, such as failing to adequately plan for a sales call. What we do know for sure is that if you believe what you conceive, personal achievement usually follows. If you convey the message that your time is valuable and important, then prospects will believe that what you have to say and to sell are valuable, too. Developing your ability and agility to work with buyers will also increase your profitability. And that's sensible selling.

The Purpose of Qualifying Is to Get the Order.

To control the buyer, of course, you need to have a full understanding of your product or service. Your company probably has invested a great deal of time and money teaching you all about what it is you are selling. If you're an automobile salesperson, for example, you probably learn about your models, fuel efficiency, aerodynamic capabilities, antilock brakes, and so on. If you sell stocks and bonds, you probably learn about financial planning, tax laws, and economic indicators. In other words, companies arm you with the hard data they believe you need to successfully sell their product or service. The questions is, is that enough? The answer in a nutshell is no.

Prospects Pay for Value.

Most salespeople fail to skyrocket to success, not because of a lack of product knowledge, but because of a lack of people knowledge. What propels successful sales representatives, in addition to product knowledge, is the ability to understand and establish rapport with buyers—all types of buyers—as well as the ability to understand, handle, and overcome those personal fears and insecurities that keep them from asking tough qualifying questions. Instead of taking action to orchestrate acceptance, unsuccessful reps perpetuate the art of avoidance. What is it they avoid? *Selling*! They find ways to avoid asking those questions that they fear could result in a no. They go out of their way to avoid feeling uncomfortable, so they practice the art of "beating around the bush" instead and ultimately are faced with answering the question "what went wrong?"

Mark Twain said, "If a cat sits on a hot stove, he will never sit on a hot stove again. But he will never sit on a cold one either. The fact is, the cat just gets out of the business of sitting on stoves!" Some salespeople are like that. They choose to leave the selling field rather than profit from lessons learned; they give in to failure rather than build for success. Salespeople who do not do what needs to be done to control the buyer become victims of circumstances, when a few critical behaviors could have transformed them into victors of circumstances instead. The salesperson who does what needs to be done to control the buyer turns people into sources of opportunities rather than into sources of frustrations. And that's sensible selling.

Self-Survey

Ask yourself if any of the following fears keep you from asking qualifying questions to prospects. Place an X in the boxes that apply to you.

- ❐ Fear of being rejected by the prospect

- ❐ Fear of embarrassing the prospect or yourself

- ❐ Fear of failing to elicit appropriate responses

- ❐ Fear of succeeding and actually having to follow through with a close

When any or all of these fears get in the way of doing your job, you, rather than the prospect, commit sales sabotage. You, rather than the prospect, erect sales barriers that prevent a successful transaction from occurring, and thus you short-circuit your sales performance.

Two key behaviors that directly contribute to sales short circuits by keeping you from controlling the buyer are (1) procrastination and (2) disorganization.

When we procrastinate, we don't do what needs to be done in a timely fashion. Why do we procrastinate? Usually because of fear, and any of the fears identified in the preceding self-survey could be the personal procrastination culprit that's limiting your performance.

Disorganization, in like fashion, is also counterproductive to successful selling. When we fail to have at our fingertips and on our lips those qualifying questions that elicit the information we need to use our time wisely and become more productive, we are disorganized. When we fail to keep track of previous discussions with prospects, or when we fail to locate data we should have on file on our prospects, again disorganization is getting in our way and might actually be destroying our ability to sell.

What's interesting is that procrastination and disorganization feed on each other. They support each other. If we conquer one, we stand a better chance of conquering the other, thereby releasing our productivity.

If You Can't Change the Price,
Change the Value That
Your Product or Service Has
For Your Prospect.

What the sensible salesperson does to control the buyer is to find out what the buyer really needs. Only when armed with that information can the salesperson give the buyer what he or she is hoping for. How do you arm yourself with that information? You ask questions and listen carefully to the answers. It's your job to find out what's on your prospect's mind and to uncover requirements and areas of dissatisfaction. If you do all the talking, the only mind you'll enter will be your own. But what's more important, you won't be able to determine the seriousness of your potential buyer, his or her desire to use your product or service, or his or her ability to purchase it.

Quality Qualifiers

How many of the following qualifying questions are part of your sales presentation? Score ten points for each X.

- If I can demonstrate how [*your product/service*] can improve productivity, quality, or profit, this is probably something you'd want to have or use. Am I correct?

- Have you considered how great it would be to increase your productivity or profit next year?

- How long have you been thinking of [*owning/using*] [*your product/ service*]?

- Who besides you will be making the decision?

- How is the purchase decision made?

- How soon do you plan on making the decision?

- What will I need to win your approval? To win the approval of others?

- If you had carte blanche, describe your ideal [*product/service*].

- What is not [*owning/using*] [*your product/service*] costing you now?

- What is keeping you from [*owning/using*] [*your product/service*] now?

- The major benefits of [*your product/service*] are [*benefits one, two, three*]. Which interests you most? Why is that? How might having that advantage solve at least one problem you're facing? What sense of urgency do you feel about solving that problem?

If you scored 80-100 percent, you understand the value of questions, and consciously or unconsciously you use questions as sales tools. When you use questions as sales tools, you help your prospects explain to themselves their reasons for buying your product or service. That's controlling the buyer. And that's sensible selling.

Establishing Needs and Wants

 ### The "Learn Needs" Script

Say eagerly, with real enthusiasm:

I'd love to learn more about your company's needs. Could you tell me how you evaluated the [*name of product/service*] you're using now?

The "Key Question" Script

Be sincere; let them know you care.

I want to help you. Before I can do that, I need to ask you a key question. If you could invent a product or service to solve all of your company's problems, what would it do?

The "Decide to Buy" Script

How did you decide to buy your last product or service? What do you like best about the product or service you are now using?

The "Major Benefits Are" Script

Know the benefits.

The major benefits this [*your product/service*] delivers are [*benefits one, two, three*]. Which interests you most? Why is that important to you? What would that do for you?

Qualifying the Buyer for Your Product or Service

 ### The "Next Step" Script

Lead prospects step by step by step.

[*Mr./Ms. Prospect*], if you believed that your company would profit by using [*your product/service*] what would be your next step?

The "How Long to Approval?" Script

A trial close.

[*Mr./Ms. Prospect*], if you felt that using [*your product/service*] would save your company time and money, how long would it take you to get the purchase approval?

The "Can You Approve?" Script

Isolate the decision maker.

[*Mr./Ms. Prospect*], can I assume that if you like [*your product/service*] and our prices, you can approve the purchase?

The "Features and Benefits" Script

What features and benefits are you most interested in?

The "Other Products" Script

What other products or services are you considering in this area?

The "Who Else?" Script

Who else are you talking to?

The "So Special" Script

Do you fully understand what makes our [*your product/service*] so special?

The "Someone Else in Decision" Script

Is someone else involved in making this decision with you?

The "Prevents" Script

Is there anything that prevents you from making a decision today?

The "Trial Close" Script

This will help you uncover any latent objections.

If our [*product/service*] meets all of your criteria or requirements, when can we [*get started/install the system/make the delivery*]?

··· **ACT III** ···

TACKLING ROADBLOCKS

Countering Objections Positively

Buyers Say the Price Is Too High
Whether They Really Believe It or Not.

How many times during your sales career have you said, "Wow, that was easy! My customers bought without raising an objection." Not too often, probably. In fact, the amount of success you experience as a salesperson relates directly to your ability to handle and overcome buyer blocks or objections. If you are ill-equipped to respond to buyer objections effectively, the only sales you'll make will be the "easy" ones, and those will be few and far between. You certainly won't get rich selling to customers who need no convincing.

Overcoming Buyer's Block: Understanding Pays

Objections pop up regularly during seller-buyer interactions. Sometimes it appears to you as if the buyer pulled the objection out of thin air. Other times you imagine the buyer working overtime in an effort to come up with a major sales block to throw your way. You can even see the buyer standing there, a half-smile on his or her face, looking at you confidently and thinking: I've got you now. That objection is more trouble than you're able to handle. Heartburn sets in. Your head throbs. And you think about changing professions. But objections are sales blocks only if you let them get in the way of a sale. Handled effectively, and answered adroitly, objections can actually help you clinch a sale. You see, if you respond to an objection appropriately, you will change the way your prospect thinks and feels about you and your product or service. Never let them see you sweat. That's sensible selling.

Now, how do you do that? Not by disagreeing with the prospect. Doing that will only antagonize him or her. Not by agreeing with the prospect. Saying that will only convince him or her of the rightness of the expressed position. So what do you do? Your job is neither to agree nor disagree; it is to understand.

"No" May Mean "Tell Me More!"

Prospects raise objections when they are unconvinced of their need for your product or service, or when they want to state an opinion different from yours. Within the objections they raise are clues to their real concerns. And behind those real concerns lie their dominant desires or fears. Thus the objections they raise help you expose and activate their hot buttons—those satisfactions they're really looking for from you, your company, and your product or service.

So when prospects raise objections or throw sales blocks straight at you, your primary goal is to let them know you understand how they feel, that if you were in their position you might well feel the same way. However, it is at this point in the conversation that you need to deflect the blocks. You need to explain to your buyers what buying or using your product or service will mean for them and their company. Thus much of your sales presentation time will be spent building a sales case around the buyer(s). Your job is to encourage your buyers to think about themselves and their relationship to your product or service. If you succeed, a sale will result. Effective sales presentations are built around buyers, they are not merely given to buyers. That means for every buyer you work with, you have to work hard to uncover what's most important to them. Once you have that information, you also have access to your buyer's personal hot button, his or her dominant desire or fear, and you can turn that hot button on again and again and again as you lead your buyer to buy and build your presentation to a successful conclusion.

The Most Important Part of Any Sales System Is the Sales Representative.

Of course, while you're attempting to build your presentation, your buyers intentionally or unintentionally are also busy building those sales blocks. Each sales block that buyers erect is an attempt at self-protection, or an effort to ensure that they are not making a mistake. Buyers, like the rest of us, are not usually risk takers. They do not want to overpay. They do not want to replace what's working. They do not want to experiment. Then what gets you over each sales block your prospect creates? What makes it possible for you to bypass those sales obstructions and convince your prospect to take action? Simply this: self-interest. Your ability to arouse and maintain buyer self-interest seriously impedes the buyer's ability to block a sale.

The key to sale making is in your hands. Turn your prospects' interests on, and you turn your prospects on to your product or service. Without turning on their interest, without activating their hot buttons, you will run head first into buyer sales block after buyer sales block, sales detour after sales detour, and eventually run out of steam. If you arouse and sustain buyer interest, however, you may still meet those sales blocks, but you'll have the fuel you need to weaken or eliminate them. You see, you convince your buyer with interest; you lose your buyer with disinterest. Either you succeed in selling your prospects on the benefits of your product or service, or your prospects succeed in selling themselves that what you have to offer is not for them. Either design your presentation with your prospects' interests in mind, or don't expect your prospects to be interested in your presentation.

If You Think Only as a Seller, You Won't Understand
the Person(s) You Are Selling To.

Each time you hit your prospects' interests, you hit their hot buttons. Each time you hit their hot buttons, you have a positive impact on their saleability.

You enhance saleability with words, images, and end results. Prospects must understand the advantages of your product or service, they must be able to visualize themselves using your product or service, and they must desire to enjoy the end result that your product or service will deliver to them. Sharing this bundle of benefits builds buying pressure in prospects and prevents them from building sales blocks for you.

So always hear out a prospect's objection. Always let the prospect tell you the whole story. Never interrupt. Never disagree. Only understand. Then and only then can you show prospects how you will help and what you will be able to do for them. Doing that takes patience. Doing that requires persistence. Doing that produces results. And that's sensible selling.

The following scripts are responses to a variety of sample objections you'll find throughout this chapter.

"The Price Is Far Too High."

The "Comparing" Script

Insist on specificity from your prospect.

What are you comparing our offering price to?

The "Consider Value" Script

The script begins with affirmation.

Price is an important consideration, isn't it? Would you consider value equally important? Let me tell you about the value of our products.

The "Planning to Pay" Script

What price were you planning on paying?

The "Price Is Why" Script

Use this script to turn the prospect's position around.

The price is exactly why you should use our [*your product/service*]. Your taste and concern for value are impeccable.

The "They Know" Script

Say, matter-of-factly:

Our competitor may know what their products are worth.

The "Easy to Swallow" Script

This script reduces the pain of price.

We can translate the price into installment payments that are easy to swallow.

The "Eliminate Options" Script

We can lower the price.

This next question arouses discontent.

What options would you like to eliminate from the package?

The "Significant Money" Script

The paraphrase is an effective tool.

What I hear you saying is that you need to be sure the product you order is cost effective. Using [*your product/service*] has saved companies like yours significant money. Let me show you why.

The "Recoup" Script

Be sure you have computed your calculations correctly.

Your investment is about [*$x*] per month—that's about [*$x*] per day and [*$x*] an hour. We estimate you'll recoup your investment in about [*number*] months, and that's not even figuring in the extra benefits you'll receive from improved employee morale.

The "Cheapest" Script

May I ask you a question? Does your company offer the cheapest prices for your [*goods/services*] in your market area?

About 90 percent of the time the answer is "no" or "not always."

We agree, then, that price is not the only consideration in making a purchase decision. The value of what you get counts too, doesn't it?

Let's talk about the values that [*your product/service*] brings with it.

The "We're Not Cheap" Script

Provide a definition of quality.

We're not cheap. We're good. I'd hate to think we offered you a [*your product/service*] with [*number*] percent more than anyone else can offer and didn't charge more for it.

The "Quality Is Costly" Script

I think you'd agree that quality is more costly. Is quality important to you?

The "What Makes You?" Script

What makes you say that? What is the reason?

The "Compared To" Script

Compared to what?

The "Comparing Us" Script

Use this to uncover the competition.

What are you comparing us to?

The "If You Don't" Script

Define the significance of your product.

What might it cost your company if you don't use our [*your product/service*]?

The "Not High Enough" Script

Our price is high. But it's not high enough when you consider the "total package" we provide.

The "If It Cost Less?" Script

If it cost less, would you use us?

If the answer is yes, continue in this way:

Good. You'd like to be able to use [*your product/service*]. Let's explore together how that can become possible.

The "Daily Cost" Script

How much is too high?

Once you have an answer, reduce it to a daily cost. Say:

That computes to [*$x*] a day over the life of the product. [*Number*] years of superior performance is worth [*$x*] a day, isn't it?

The "Why Hesitating?" Script

You can refer to personal preferences effectively to build rapport.

You're obviously a person who appreciates value. Why are you hesitating to buy what you need now? Would you seek the services of an attorney who charged $5 an hour or a surgeon who charged a flat fee of $100 per procedure?

Why would you want to scrimp on quality now? Your company deserves the best [*product/service*] available.

The "Feel and Found" Script

This is a common, well-established, workable sales sequence.

I know how you feel. At times I felt that way myself. Do you know what I found?

The next few scripts isolate the problem.

The "Only Money?" Script

Is it *only* a matter of money?

The "Only Thing?" Script

Is that the *only thing* holding you back?

These next scripts are trial closes.

The "Resolve the Cost" Script

I appreciate your honesty. If we can resolved the cost to your satisfaction, then would you want to purchase it today?

The "More Than Fair" Script

If I can demonstrate that the price is more than fair and our [*product/service*] is worth every cent we are asking, would you permit yourself to take advantage of what I am offering today?

The "Convince Yourself" Script

If you can convince yourself that the price is more than fair, would you be in a position to proceed with a yes decision today?

The "Tough to Overpay" Script

Do you like our [*product/service*]?

> *If the prospect says yes, which is frequently the case, with qualifications regarding the cost, then ask:*

Wouldn't you concur that it is tough to overpay for what you really like?

The "Quality Concerns You Every Day" Script

> *This clears away the smokescreen and neutralizes the prospect.*

Price concerns you today. Quality concerns you every day. Aren't you better off paying a little more than you expected rather than a lot less than you need to ensure quality?

If you pay a little more now, over the life of [*your product/service*] we're talking cents. If, however, you pay less than you should and what you end up with creates rather than alleviates problems, we're talking trouble with a capital *T*.

Not being willing to pay for quality could end up being very costly, wouldn't you agree?

The "Price or Cost" Script

Notice the difference in word use.

Is it the price or the *cost* that concerns you? You see, you pay the price only once—when you purchase. Cost, however, is of concern for as long as you [*own/use*] the [*product/service*]. You might find a lower price out there; you won't find a lower cost.

Since you strike me as a cost-conscious decision maker, can you think of any reason why your company shouldn't take advantage of the lowest possible cost?

The "We Win the War" Script

Compliments the prospect sincerely.

I'm glad to see price concerns you, because that is where we win the war. Would you agree that a product or service is worth what it does for you, not what you have to expend to own or use it?

Let's explore what benefits our [*product/service*] offers you.

The "A Year From Now" Script

You need to be personally convinced and professionally convincing to use this.

A year from now price won't concern you if [*your product/service*] lives up to your expectations. However, even if you pay less, you'll constantly be reminded of the cost of poor performance, inferior service, or lack of quality. It ends up being what you paid for.

I'd rather have you convince yourself of the value we're offering you today, at a price that allows us to deliver you value, than to have to say "I'm sorry" over and over because of poor performance or inferior or lack of quality for years to come. That is sensible, isn't it?

The "Cost per Day" Script

Minimize price to its smallest component.

[*Mr./Ms. Prospect*], how many years do you figure you will [*own/use*] [*your product/service*]?

Okay. Let's take [*number*] years, and if [*your product/service*] only costs [*$x*] more, it is costing you [*$x*] per year for the best you can find in the industry. Since there are 365 days in a year, you are talking about [*number of cents/dollars*] per day for the finest product or service available. Now, that's a pretty fair offer, isn't it?

The "High Quality Not Cheap" Script

High quality products or services are not cheap, and cheap products or services are not of high quality.

Our company had a choice. We could either design our [*product/service*] to do as little as possible so we could sell it for a pittance, or we could design it to do as much as possible so that over many years your cost would be lower than otherwise.

"The "Invest in the Best" Script

[*Mr./Ms. Prospect*], don't you agree it makes more sense to invest in the best now than to pay for something that is ultimately inferior?

The "Value Is in What It Will Do for You" Script

Alleviates skepticism.

[*Mr./Ms. Prospect*], the value of our [*product/service*] is what it will do for you, not what you have to pay for it. If it brings you big benefits and helps alleviate pressing problems, then it is a bargain, isn't it?

The "Headaches" Script

We especially like this one!

If you think [*your product/service*] costs too much, how will you pay for all the problems, *headaches*, and expenses that will result from not using us?

"I Need to Check Out Your Competitors."

 ### The "Their Specifications" Script

Come prepared!

That's no problem. I have their specifications right here. What do you need to know to make this decision?

The "Why Concerned?" Script

Probe for the real objection.

Why? What is it that concerns you?

The "What Could Prevent?" Script

Ask for feedback.

Is there anything that I've shared with you that could prevent you from giving us the opportunity to serve you?

The "Compare Competitors" Script

Diffuse the argument and generate trust with the prospect.

That's good. What criteria will you be using when you do that? Please share with me which competitors you are considering. I can help you compare the features and benefits of their [*products/services*] with ours.

The "They Did Your Homework" Script

Give yourself a situational advantage. After all, you are the expert.

I understand that. Many of our current customers also used that strategy. In many ways they did your homework for you. Let's go over what they found out and why they elected to go with us.

The "Let's Compare" Script

Good. Whose [*products/services*] are you also considering? Let's compare and contrast those features and benefits you're hoping to find with what we have to offer.

The "Strong Points" Script

I understand. You need to consider the assets each will provide. Based on what you now know about us, will you share with me what you believe are our strong points, and/or our weaknesses?

The "Consultant/Expert" Script

I would expect you to make comparisons. Most educated buyers do that. In fact, let's examine the [*products/services*] most frequently recommended by [*names of companies*].

The "I Compare Options" Script

Propose a specific line of action.

You feel you need more information before deciding, don't you? That's understandable. I compare options daily for the clients I serve. I'll gladly answer any questions you pose. That will save you time and effort. I know you'll be more comfortable making a decision after we go over your questions.

The "Need To?" Script

Communicate surprise.

Need to? When was the last time you bought something without comparing choices?

The "Apples and Oranges" Script

Set up the image.

Are we comparing apples and oranges? Is it really fair to compare us to [*your competition*]? Our firm is the diamond of our industry. Please don't try to compare us to a cubic zirconia.

"We Have Decided Not to Buy the Product/Service from You."

 ### *The "Why?" Script*

May I ask why?

The "What Changed?" Script

What changed your mind?

The "Still Time to Change" Script

Who did you decide to go with?

> *Wait for an answer.*

They are a good company, but, of course, we feel we are better because [*your company's benefit*].

I'm sure that there is still time to change your mind, isn't there?

The "Where Did I Go Wrong?" Script

> *Ask for feedback.*

What caused you to make that decision? Obviously, I failed to get my message across. Could you share with me where I went wrong?

The "No Longer Concerned" Script

> *Remind the prospect of worthy objectives. Create pain.*

Are you no longer concerned with [*improving productivity/enhancing morale/increasing profits*]?

The "Today or Ever?" Script

Focus on buyer behavior.

Today or ever? "Today" I can reluctantly accept. "Forever" leaves me very disturbed. It was my impression that helping your company effectively prepare for the future was a top priority, and I am fully committed to helping you accomplish that. What is keeping that from happening?

The "Must Be a Reason" Script

[*Mr./Ms. Prospect*], I see you feel quite strongly about this, so there must be a reason for your feeling as you do. I'd appreciate it if you'd share that reason with me.

The "Feedback" Script

It is with your feedback that we can continually improve. What did you prefer about [*competition company's product/service*]?

If we were to bid for your business again, where would you suggest we focus improvement efforts?

"Times Are Tough."

 ### *The "Get Through" Script*

Change the focus.

That makes this the perfect time to talk. Our [*your product/service*] is designed to help companies like yours get through the tough times.

The "Improve the Situation" Script

A foundation builder.

Our [*your product/service*] will improve your situation.

The "Increase Profits" Script

Tough times call for you to be able to increase profits. Using [*your product/service*] can help you do that.

The "Minimize the Negative" Script

We couldn't agree more that the economy is making times tough for everyone—even us!

In fact, we have designed the pricing of our [*products/services*] to minimize the negative impact of these times and actually reduce your cost basis.

The "Meet the Challenges" Script

Make it hard to say no.

[*Your product/service*] can help you meet the challenges that tough times present you with. It's important for you to emerge from today's challenges stronger, isn't it?

The "Difficult Decisions" Script

Maximize the risk of inaction.

Difficult times mean you'll have to make difficult decisions. Let's be sure that this decision won't hurt productivity or profit.

The "Weather the Storm" Script

If times are tough, it doesn't make sense to limit your ability to weather the storm. Why not limit your order instead of not placing one at all? That also limits your risk.

The "Withholding Medicine" Script

Analogies can help; try this one.

You can't keep a patient healthy by withholding medicine that's required. The same holds true for a business.

It's not healthy to cut back on those purchases that could enhance your ability to make it through the rough period. Doing that could make it impossible for you to be a force to be reckoned with when good times return. Let's work through this tough period together.

The "Market Share" Script

Create pain and provide a cure.

Not placing an order could adversely affect your market share. Instead of strengthening your position in the market, your inaction could weaken it. Let's take action to secure your future instead.

The "Lower Costs" Script

Tough times make it even more important that you look at ways to lower costs and increase profits. We can help you accomplish both. Let me show you how.

"We Feel We Must Be Loyal to Our Current Supplier."

 ### The "Respect Loyalty" Script

Get things in proper perspective.

I respect your sense of loyalty to my competitor. I believe in loyalty as well. I think that your first loyalty should be to the well-being of your own company, don't you?

The "If Ours Is Better" Script

Boil it down.

If I can show you that our [*product/service*] is better for your company than the one you are currently using, you would consider changing, or at least sampling ours, wouldn't you?

The "Worth the Change?" Script

Make it hard to say no.

Would it be worth the change in loyalty for a [*cost reduction/increase in morale/increase in productivity*]?

The "Times Change" Script

Encourage the prospect to take a fresh look.

Times change. You really have grown beyond your present situation.

The "Make Exceptions?" Script

Everyone makes exceptions now and then, so ask!

Do you ever make exceptions? Just suppose we could [*improve prof-its/boost productivity/reduce turnover*], you would want to consider us then, wouldn't you?

The "You Deserve Better" Script

I understand your sense of loyalty. However, you do deserve to have a better [*product/service*].

The "Worth the Trouble?" Script

Promise something more.

Wouldn't it be worth the trouble of changing to [*your company*] to be able to be recognized as a leader in the marketplace?

The "There Has Been Progress" Script

I certainly can understand wanting to stay with a solution you feel is the best around.

Remember that not long ago manual typewriters were considered state of the art; then came electric typewriters, then electronic type-writers, then PCs, now workstations.

I would like to have the opportunity to show you how we can take you from a system that works sufficiently to one that brings you true cost savings and productivity. Let me introduce you to our solution on [*day*], or would [*another day*] be better?

"We Use Another Company's Product/Service and Do Not Need You at this Time."

 ### The "What Is Keeping You?" Script

Word emphasis is critical here.

What is *keeping you* from selecting a *better* [*product/service*]?

The "I'm Surprised" Script

Gives you time to rethink the approach.

I'm surprised to hear you say that. Please share your reasons with me.

The "Not Totally Happy?" Script

Helps overcome intransigence.

Is there anything about your present situation you're not totally happy with? Just suppose our [*your product/service*] could eliminate that problem. It would be worth considering then, wouldn't it?

The "Why They Switched" Script

Stories sell.

Some of our best customers today used to use our competition yesterday. Let me tell you why they switched to us.

The "Who Would?" Script

Open a new door.

Perhaps you don't. Could you suggest someone in your organization who would?

The "How Many Suppliers?" Script

Help prospect break free of ties that bind.

How many of the suppliers that you did business with ten years ago do you still do the same amount of business with today?

The "What Do They Do?" Script

Help the prospect assess the situation.

Would you share with me what you believe your present supplier does best? Could you tell me what you feel they could improve on?

The "Small Order" Script

Minimize the risk.

I understand. But why not give us a try on a small [*order/job*]? Check us out and see how we can benefit you.

The "Opportunity" Script

I admire your loyalty. Wouldn't you agree that you also owe loyalty to your company to help increase profits and improve performance? This might be such an opportunity.

The "Admirable" Script

Your loyalty to your vendor is admirable. But so is loyalty to your company's long-term future.

Wouldn't you agree that that kind of loyalty is as critical as loyalty to a vendor? If I can show you how to enhance your company's future picture, you'd take a serious look at what we have to offer, wouldn't you?

The "Doubly Hard" Script

A credibility builder.

I appreciate your telling me that. Now I have to work doubly hard to earn your business.

The "They Told Me" Script

Say proudly:

That's just about what every one of my present customers told me the first time I called. Why do you suppose that I count them among my best customers now?

The "Give Us a Chance" Script

Use the paraphrase.

What I hear you saying is that the reason you aren't using us is that we aren't currently working together. Why not give us a chance to prove our worth to you?

The "Road of Least Effort" Script

The prospect must assess the cost of failure.

I understand. The road of least effort is the road of no action. But no action can lead to no growth. I think if you give a little more consideration to how [*your product/service*] compares with [*your competition*], you'll see what I'm talking about. Let's compare those features and benefits now.

The "If Nothing Else" Script

Well, if for nothing else but to reaffirm that your decision and your relationship with your current supplier is the best for you, let's meet for twenty minutes to give you a basis of comparison.

The "Status Quo" Script

I understand. Many of our present clients were also content with the status quo. However, when they fully understood what we had to offer, that contentment disappeared. You'd agree that it's important to stay informed, wouldn't you?

Let me tell you why other companies took action and switched to us.

The "Change Again" Script

History can work for you today.

What did you use before using your present company's [*product/ service*]? What made you change to your new supplier? Let me show you why it now makes good sense to change again.

The "Change Is Necessary" Script

Change is never comfortable, is it? But let me show you why change is necessary if you're going to have an advantage over your competition.

The "Change Is Difficult" Script

I understand. Change is difficult. But if we were always content to maintain the status quo, we would not make the kind of progress we're capable of.

The "Smart Companies" Script

Hard to disagree with this one.

You'd agree that smart companies are always on the lookout for ways to improve and prosper, wouldn't you? Forward-looking companies don't sit still. You don't believe in sitting still either, do you?

Let me share with you how our [*products/services*] can help you take another leap forward and improve your market position.

The "Alternative Source" Script

I understand and I respect your loyalty. But it makes good business sense to have an alternative source. Why not try us out with a small order?

The "Show You" Script

Focus, focus.

I see. What would I need to show you in order to change your mind?

The "Explore Possibilities" Script

Watch emphasis.

I understand your present vendor is meeting your performance standards *at this time.* I feel, nonetheless, that it would be worth fifteen minutes of our time to meet and explore the possibilities so that should circumstances change, you'd be prepared to take positive action.

The "How Did You Decide?" Script

How did you decide to use [*their present supplier*]?

The "If There Were a Way?" Script

[*Mr./Ms. Prospect*], if there were a way you could buy the same product, at a better price, and get better service, you'd want to know how to do that, wouldn't you?

The "Not Asking for All Business" Script

Stress is key here.

I'm not asking for *all* of your business. I'm simply asking that you give me the *opportunity to earn part* of your business.

Since I know you feel obligated to [*your competitor*], doesn't it make sense that *I'll work harder and provide better service*, just to earn that opportunity? Could we start you with [*order*], or would [*larger order*] be better?

The "Add to Your Business" Script

A really effective soft sell.

I understand and I appreciate your position. I don't want you to take business away from [*your competitor*] so you can give it to me. However, I have ideas that will add to the business you do. If I share those ideas with you, will you agree to give me the extra business built by the ideas? That's fair, isn't it?

The *"Just Like Theirs"* Script

Start with agreement.

I see. You feel our product is just like theirs. There are a number of similarities between us and our competitor. And there are a number of important differences, too.

Let me show you the differences that help us stand out and excel. You are interested in excelling, too, aren't you?

"We Don't Want to Risk Changing."

 ### The "Three Things That Please You" Script

I appreciate that. That's a real nice position for your present [*supplier/ vendor*] to be in. I wonder if you'd share with me the three things that please you most about *him/her*].

The prospect's answer, in effect, describes the benefits you need to top or acknowledge. Respond in this way:

Now, what are three things you'd like to see improved?

The prospect's answer reveals the gaps you can fill. Respond in this way:

Yes. I can see why improving [*the three weaknesses mentioned*] would be important to you. Lots of problems develop when [*the three weaknesses*] are not addressed.

The "Is Ours Better?" Script

The question is, is our [*product/service*] so much better that you need to consider it? That is the question, isn't it?

The "What If We Deserved?" Script

Be sure to smile when you ask.

What if you believed we also deserved that kind of loyalty? If that were the case, could you see how our [*product/service*] would be one you'd want?

The "We Must Determine" Script

What we must determine, then, is if our firm offers the benefits and personal attention that will create long-term loyalty. Don't we?

The "Second Supplier" Script

Why not try us out by using us as a second supplier?

The "Don't Chance Anything" Script

I'm not suggesting you chance anything. What you need is [*superior service/increased profit/improved productivity*].

It will take fifteen minutes for you to decide if I have what you need. The calendar shows that [*day*] at [*time*] is good, or would [*another day/time*] be better for you?

The "Most Important" Script

Be inquisitive. Ask:

What can I do to become your most important supplier of [*your product/service*]?

"Your Company Is Too Large/Small."

The "Volume Keeps Costs Down" Script

Acknowledge the prospect's position.

Yes, we are a large company, and you'll benefit directly from our sales volume, which lets us keep costs down. Keeping costs down is important to you, isn't it?

The "We've Grown It" Script

Yes, our company is large, and we've grown it one service-oriented person at a time. In fact, we pride ourselves on the personal attention we give each of our customers.

Personal attention is important to you, isn't it?

The "Attention to Your Needs" Script

Yes, and that's a direct benefit to you. Our size permits us to pay careful attention to your needs at the same time that it lets us give you unparalleled personal service. Real personal service is tough to find these days, isn't it?

The "I Am Driven" Script

I am measured by how satisfied my customer base is. That is how I am paid, and how my performance is reviewed. So I, personally, as well as our support staff, are driven to ensure that you are totally satisfied. We have enough staff to make that support a reality.

"We Can Buy It for Less Money Elsewhere."

 ### The "Price and Value" Script

Isolate and substitute.

Is price your most important consideration? Most business people consider value equally important. Would you agree with that assessment? Let me share why [*your product/service*] offers the best value.

The "Their Worth" Script

Exercise caution here.

If our competitors charge less, what does that tell you about the real worth of what they're selling?

The "Imitations Versus Original" Script

I see. You can buy many imitations for less than you'd pay for an original. What you need to consider, however, is whether the results you'll achieve will also be poor imitations of what might otherwise have been valuable benefits. That does concern you at least somewhat, doesn't it?

The "Attorney or Physician" Script

Emphasis is critical to the persuasiveness in this one.

When you need an attorney or a physician, do you base your decision regarding your choice *solely* on how much they *charge*? You'd also be concerned with *reputation*, *level of expertise*, and *service*, wouldn't you?

Shouldn't this decision be made in the same way? Let's consider the quality of what we're offering now.

The "Invest in Quality" Script

Work the numbers.

How much less? How long do you expect the [*product/service*] to last? That means for only [*$x*] more per day, you could afford to have the best [*product/service*]. That's not too much to invest in order to have quality too, is it?

The "Low Price Versus Poor Quality" Script

Be sure to emphasize contrasts.

Which is more important to you—that the [*product/service*] you select be *low in price or high in quality*? What good is a low price if quality is absent?

The "What Are They Omitting?" Script

Introspection is the key here. Encourage the prospect to question, too.

Yes. [*Your competition*] does offer a lower price. I wonder what they're omitting.

The "I'm Not Crazy" Script

If I could get the same product for less, I would definitely buy it! I'm not crazy. However, I am not aware of any other company selling the *same* product for any price.

They may claim to have *similar* features; let me take this opportunity to compare.

"We Tried That Before and It Didn't Work."

 ### The "Why Different?" Script

Say with surprise in your voice:

That's interesting. Have you any ideas why [*the company you are talking to*] is different from most of the others in the same field you're in?

The "Bad Experience" Script

Say sympathetically:

It sounds like you've had a bad experience with a similar [*product/ service*]. Would you share it with me?

The "Progress" Script

A lot of progress has been made in a very short time. Wouldn't it make sense to base a purchase decision on today's offering and conditions, not yesterday's?

The "Wrong?" Script

What went wrong?

The "Like Giving Up Eating" Script

The ability to empathize is key here.

I'm sorry to hear that. I know how disappointing it is to buy something and then be sorry you did. But we can't give up buying because we had a bad experience. That's like giving up eating in all restaurants because the food in one was disappointing.

Let me share with you how the experience you'll have working with us will be different.

The "What Caused?" Script

Isolate the problem.

What exactly caused the problem—the product or the service? The company? The support?

The "We're Different From" Script

I think we may be comparing apples and oranges. What we do is totally different from [*what they tried*]. Let me show you how we're different and why we're better.

The "Disappointments" Script

Stress common concerns.

I understand. We've all experienced disappointments, haven't we? I hope that one bad experience hasn't turned you off so badly that you're hesitant to make the most of a promising opportunity. That's what we're offering right now. Let me explain.

"It Sounds Risky."

 ### The "Assessment" Script

Say inquisitively:

May I ask what you're basing that assessment on?

The "Compared" Script

Compared to what?

The "Riskier" Script

Turn it around; use emphasis.

It may be riskier for you *not* to use our [*product/service*]. What is the value you place on improved [*productivity/performance/morale*]?

The "Ever Glad?" Script

Ask curiously:

Were you ever glad you took a chance and won? This will be one of those days, too. Use the opportunity.

I would like to show you how a decision to go with our company is actually risk free.

"Your Company Is New on the Block; You Have No Track Record."

 ### The "We Took the Best" Script

We are new. We are innovative. We are customer-oriented. We "stole shamelessly" from all the big companies. We applied lessons learned and we have designed a new [*product/service*] for you.

We have a lot to prove—a lot at stake, so believe me, we will be sure that all our clients judge us as the best.

We can't afford to rest on our laurels or take any customer for granted.

The "New" Script

Ask for definition.

What do you consider new?

The "Count on Us" Script

Reversals work.

That's the reason why you can count on us.

The "Initial Advantage" Script

Establish common bonds.

Every company was new at one time. Those who get on board early save money. Why not be one of those who have the initial advantage?

The "You Were New" Script

Puts prospect in your shoes.

Your company was new at one time, too. Isn't our [*product/service*] in the same position you were in at that time?

Doesn't it make good sense to consider the benefits we have to offer? Let's do that now.

The "Ever Worked With New?" Script

Has your company ever worked with a new company and profited from it? That's just the opportunity you're faced with now.

Handling Stalls

The Psychology of Stalling: It's Decision Time

When prospects come close to placing an order or making a buying decision, it's normal for them to react somewhat fearfully, to look for reasons to postpone making the actual decision, and to try to buy time so they can either seek confirmation from others or convince themselves via self-talk that what they are considering doing is right. When these natural reactions occur, your task is to help them explore the possibilities, emphasize the benefits to them of what you're selling so that you fuel their desire and interest, and give them the leeway they need to ponder the purchase safely. Never give potential purchasers the impression that you find their doubts or concerns silly. Instead, let them feel you're working with them to discover the solution that's best for them. What you do, in effect, is to work with them to realize benefits and avoid consequences. If customers let their fear of consequences overpower their desire for benefits, they will not take action. So your job is clear: Without belittling their fears, you need to help them refocus their perspective. You need to replace their concern for consequences with an obsession for benefits. You accomplish this by focusing their concentration on outcomes of ownership that will reward rather than punish them.

Try this: Once you know all the advantages your product offers, sit at your desk with two blank sheets of paper in front of you. At the top of sheet 1 write "Buyer Gains," and at the top of sheet 2 write "Buyer Loses." Next, list all the possible gains your product or service will bring its buyers on sheet 1, and on sheet 2 list all those things buyers will lose or forfeit if they fail to purchase your product or service.

Planning Is Important,
But It Can't Replace Action.

Prospects turn into purchasers because they want something or because they want to avoid something. They stall when they aren't sure if what you're offering them will actually alleviate a problem they want solved, provide a sure-fire means to help them look good, or absolutely enable them to avoid looking bad. Most people want to be alive, to feel secure, to be liked, to feel important. You can use these wants to help people justify buying your product or service. When they put up a stop sign, it may be because their motivation to buy at this time is too low. Their doubts may be due to price, what others will think, whether the product or service will do the job, or if this is the best time to make the purchase. So your job becomes one of demonstrating that the purchase is worth its price, that others will think well of their decision, that now is the best time to purchase, because the product or service will do the job or solve a problem. Though neither you nor they may realize it, prospects look to you for justification, and you can help. Predecisional anxiety (indecision) is painful, and your goal is to see that it's not prolonged. The longer it festers, the more difficult buying becomes. So take action to rescue your prospects from the grip of indecision by taking away the hurt they imagine and substituting in its place one of their key wants.

Try this: Divide a sheet of paper in half. Label the left half "My Concerns." Label the right half "Your Rewards." Ask the prospect to list those reasons that are preventing him or her from taking action. Then you list all the benefits that taking action will precipitate.

Remember, prospects value benefits. Benefits, not selling techniques, overcome prospect indecision. If you have to interest your prospects in your product, you haven't really discovered what interests them. If you haven't discovered what interests them, you can't possibly know how your product or service will satisfy their interests. Consequently, to stop stalls you need to know what your prospects want and why they want it. That's sensible selling. If your product can't answer what and why questions satisfactorily, if your product can't provide enough justification for the prospect's purchase, then the stall will be transformed from an objection you can handle to the overt rejection of your product or service.

The following scripts are responses to a variety of sample stalls you'll find throughout this chapter.

"We Want to Think It Over."

 ### The "Great" Script

This is a fun response!

Great! What do we need to think about?

The "Phone Call" Script

This gives prospects a little breathing room.

Fine. I'll just make a phone call while you folks talk it over, and then I'll be right back to answer any question you may have.

The "Have a Reason" Script

Cut to the heart of the problem.

You must have a reason for saying that. I'd like to know what it is.

The "Small Decision" Script

Put things in perspective.

This is a relatively small decision for you, isn't it? Why not just make your decision now and get on to other things? I will then be able to handle this project for you.

The "More Time" Script

Why do you need to invest even more time in making this decision?

The "Holding Back" Script

Use this when other techniques have not worked.

Would you please share with me what it is that is really holding you back from making this decision?

The "Time and Energy" Script

Let's go ahead and get this started. Is it really worth any more of your valuable time and energy?

The "Let's Picture" Script

This script carries the prospect from the thinking mode to the visual mode.

I see. I also can picture the problems you're currently facing with [*lean profits/employee turnover/low morale*]. Right? Our [*your product/service*] can help solve that problem. Now let's picture this together.

Four to six months go by. Your CEO is looking at roughs of the annual report. [*He/she*] calls to congratulate you for the steps you took to get [*profits/turnover/morale*] under control. Now that's the kind of picture you'd like to appear in, isn't it?

Whether you're in that picture depends on the action you're about to take. Let's develop the best picture possible together and turn possibility into reality.

The "Persistent Problems" Script

I understand how you feel. I also understand those persistent problems that brought us together in the first place—[*low profits/low morale/poor service*]. Keep those in your mind's eye. That's not the kind of scene you want to keep replaying week after week, is it? If you take action to solve those problems today, your associates will thank you tomorrow.

Can't you see yourself being thanked by [*your boss/your peers*] for having made it possible for them to achieve even greater success? Why not start to turn that image into reality today?

The "Think Together" Script

Show concern with this one.

Let's think things through together. What exactly are you concerned about?

The "Thinking Makes Sense" Script

Show enthusiasm.

That's good. Thinking about ways to improve productivity and profits is necessary and makes lots of sense. We agree that taking action to accomplish those goals is also important.

Let's talk about how [*your product/service*] can help.

The "Not Clearly Communicated" Script

You can take the blame if it gets the order!

I hear you. You're telling me that I haven't clearly communicated the advantages you'll gain from using [*your product/service*]. If I had communicated clearly, you wouldn't still be thinking, you'd be taking positive action.

What is it that requires clarification?

The "Think Too Long" Script

The prospect must understand the consequences of inaction.

Sometimes when we think too long, we pass up a real opportunity. Let's be sure this is one opportunity you take advantage of. To make sure procrastination doesn't cost you more, can we take positive action and authorize the paperwork now?

The "Easier Work" Script

Just think how much easier work will become if you buy [*your product/service*].

The "Best Decision" Script

Get the prospect sharing with you.

Tell me about the best decision you ever made to use a [*product/ service*] offered you. How did you do it? How did you make up your mind to buy or use [*product/service*]?

After the prospect replies, you say:

Well, I believe you made a wise decision then, and I also believe you'll make an even wiser decision now.

The "Main Concern" Script

What is the main concern you have left?

The "What Would It Take?" Script

What would it take for you to order our [*product/service*] right now? [*More discounts/better delivery time/another color/options thrown in*]?

The "Special" Script

Do you fully understand what makes our [*your product/service*] so special?

The "Need to Do" Script

A great closer!

What would I need to do to sell you our [*your product/service*] now?

The "You Would Not Waste Time" Script

Become excited!

That's super! I know you wouldn't waste your time thinking about it if it did not interest you. So I assume you want to think it over so you don't make a mistake as you make a yes or no decision.

What you want to do is make the right decision, isn't that so?

To make the right decision, you need all the facts. Why don't we think together for a few moments. Let's start with these questions:

- Do you like our [*product/service*]?
- Do you want to [*own/use*] our [*product/service*]?
- Can you afford to purchase our [*product/service*]?
- When would you like to start enjoying the benefits of [*your product/service*]?

Now, is there anything else you need to think about?

"We Are Going to Wait Until the Next Quarter."

 ### The "Firm Order" Script

The assumptive close often works.

Then your order is firm. Great! Let's fill out the paperwork, and we will ship on the first day of the next quarter.

The "Delay Billing" Script

Make a concession.

I have an even better idea. Why don't we ship today and delay the billing until the first of the next quarter? That way you can start getting the benefit of our [*product/service*] right away.

The "Why Delay?" Script

Say with astonishment:

Why would you want to delay an important decision like this one?

Let's get things rolling today!

The "Timing Is Important" Script

I understand. Timing can be important. Why do you want to buy then and not now?

The "Put Off?" Script

Why put off making this decision?

The "Hope to Gain?" Script

Focus on the pain of indecision.

Let's see if I can help. What do you hope to gain by waiting? What might you lose by waiting?

The "Put Heads Together" Script

How do you expect things to change by next quarter? Perhaps by putting our heads together we can solve your problems today.

The "Take Action" Script

Compliment the prospect.

I perceive you as someone who is willing to take action when the situation calls for it. What additional information do you need to support [*hiring us/buying from us*] today?

The "Lose Competitive Edge" Script

The image of loss is powerful.

I understand you need more time to think. But if during the time you're thinking you lose your competitive edge in the marketplace, that could be very, very costly to you.

Why not make the decision now and act to enhance your market position instead?

The "Medical Attention" Script

Encourages role taking.

When someone you really care about needs medical attention, what do you do? You get that person to a doctor as soon as possible, don't you? Put that decision off, and you take a very big risk.

We're in a similar situation here. Your company needs our [*your product/service*] at this time. Let's get moving now.

The "Paperwork Now" Script

A good close!

Your plan is to purchase next quarter? Let's fill out the paperwork now, and we'll [*ship/get started*] the day you select.

"Business Is Really Slow Right Now."

The "Prioritize" Script

Put the pressure on.

I understand. You must prioritize your purchases right now. Let me show you why our [*product/service*] must be at the top of your list in order for you to compete successfully in the difficult times that lie ahead.

The "Testimony" Script

Let the failure of others work for you, but be careful. This can be perceived as threatening.

Let me tell you a story about one of our customers who cut out our [*product/service*] when the going got rough. [*He/she*] is no longer in the business, whereas [*his/her*] competition prospered.

The "Cut Back" Script

Maybe you should cut back on the size of the order. Do you really want to eliminate our [*product/service*] completely?

The "Starving" Script

Seek a concession.

Cutting back is one thing. Starving is something else, isn't it?

The "Increase" Script

Would you like to increase profits?

The "Waiting Costs" Script

That's exactly why we should meet as soon as possible. Waiting any longer could cost your company a lot of money.

The "Not Your Intention" Script

I'm sure it's not your intention to allow that to continue. Let's go over how we can help improve your business situation.

The "Turn Around" Script

That's why we're here. Let's discuss how we can help you turn things around.

The "Positive Action" Script

If business is slow, you need to take positive action now to increase [*productivity/performance/morale*]. Let's talk about how we can help you accomplish that.

The "Competition Plan" Script

Use role taking to change prospect thinking.

How do you think your competition responds when their business slows? They don't damage their ability to grow.

Prioritizing purchases is important. Terminating purchases that could positively affect your company's survival ability is dangerous. Let's explore why it's important for you to own [*your product/ service*] now.

The "Proper Positioning" Script

> *Promote interest in prospect's goal.*

That may be true. But if you cut back during the tough times, you may not be positioned properly to react quickly enough to changes when the times turn around. Is proper positioning important to you? We're ready to help you establish a good market position.

"We're Not Ready to Buy."

 ### The "Your Thinking" Script

Persistence will pay, so ask!

What's your thinking regarding when you will be ready to make a decision to buy?

The "Critical Factors" Script

What were the critical factors you considered when deciding?

The "Needs to Happen" Script

Another great closer!

What needs to happen for you to be able to justify a buying decision now?

The "Appreciate Honesty" Script

I understand and I appreciate your honesty.

What makes you say that?

"I Need to Share This With My Boss."

 ### The "Introduce the Boss" Script

Take control.

Great! Why don't you just introduce [*him/her*] to me, and let me do the work? That's what I'm paid to do.

The "Small Item" Script

Hard sell. Be careful.

Are you sure that you really want to bother your superior with such a small item? Shouldn't we just get things started?

The "Talk About" Script

What do you need to talk to [*him/her*] about?

The "We'll Talk" Script

That's a great deal! When can we talk to [*him/her*]? Is [*he/she*] available right now?

The "Is Boss Involved?" Script

Who else is part of the decision-making process? Is your boss involved in all purchase decisions?

If the prospect's answer is yes, continue in this way:

Let's set up a time for us to get together with [*him/her*].

If the prospect's answer is no, continue in this way:

What makes this purchase decision different from others?

The "Boss Plus" Script

Get the prospect working with you.

Who in addition to your boss will be making the decision with you? Now that you're favorably impressed, can I count on you to accompany me so I can present these benefits to [*your boss/anyone else involved in the purchase decision*]?

The "Prevents You" Script

What prevents you from making the decision now?

··· **ACT IV** ···

WRAPPING IT UP!

Closing Successfully

Take the *C* Out of *Close* and You *Lose*

Selling Is the Only Way to Reduce
the Cost of Doing Business.

Closing needs to be a natural part of the selling process. At any point in the salesperson-prospect exchange, the prospect may signal that he or she wants to own your product or service. Whenever that occurs, you need to be ready to close. Waste that opportunity and you could sacrifice the sale. The *C* in *close* stands for consummation; when you take the *C* away, you're left with *lose*. Who loses? Both you and your customer do. You lose because you had a customer who was ready to buy. You had a customer who was excited by what you had to offer, who perceived an end to a problem situation, who understood the potential benefits and was able to envision what was in it for him or her. But because you failed to consummate the dialogue between you and the prospect appropriately, you let all that slip away. Your customer also loses because the natural conclusion, his or her expected result, was taken away, and he or she was taken from anticipation to indecision.

Thus, when you had the opportunity to take a giant step forward, you took two or more giant steps backward—you did not seize the moment and close. For all these reasons, it's essential that you close every time the opportunity to do so is there.

Closing a Sale Is
a Far Better Feeling
Than Being Close to a Sale.

Trial closes let you determine how close you're getting to closing. They also help you diagnose buyer desire and urgency. When you use a trial close, you take your prospect's buying temperature and you test your prospect's buying potential. You also gain valuable information.

Which of these trial closes do you use regularly?

- How long have you been considering owning [*your product/service*]?

- How do you feel about [*your product/service*]?

- What do you think of [*your product/service*]?

- In your opinion, would you want to use the [*one version*] or the [*another version*] of [*your product/service*]?

- If you were to make a positive decision, would you feel better with the [*one version*] or the [*another version*] of [*your product/service*]?

- On a scale of 1 to 10, with 10 being ready to purchase, where are you?

- In order to attain your goals, would it be worth an investment of [*cost of your product/service*]?

Each of the answers to the preceding questions lets you know what your prospect thinks about your product or service. Only if you know what your prospect is thinking can you plan your presentation sequence effectively. Your trial closing ability is directly related to your ability to gauge how much your prospect wants your product or service at a specific point in time. A trial close can flush out concerns or areas of weakness in your presentation. For example, if you find that your prospect's commitment level is low, then you know you haven't conveyed sufficient benefits for him or her to want to own your product or service. The prospect isn't "wanting" enough. When you control prospect want, you control the sale. If your prospect isn't ready to buy, a hasty closing could actually push you further apart. Even the best salesperson can't close a prospect who doesn't want what he or she has to offer. And it is the prospect's reactions to your trial closes that let you know how close you are to succeeding, or the extent to which your prospect can picture him- or herself owning and benefiting from your offering.

Effective Closing Is the Mother of Effective Selling.
Behind Every Effective Sale Is an Effective Salesperson.

How do you know if your prospects are ready to buy? You look for buying signals and you test desire. When a prospect shows interest, that's a buying signal. As prospects consider what it would be like to own or use your product or service, their ways of relating to you change. They may lean forward, strike a thinking pose, become more animated, relax, become friendlier, or ask you a series of questions about your product or service. When this happens, their SQ (seriousness quotient) is up, and your TCQ (trial closing quotient) needs to rise accordingly.

If You Don't Know How to Close,
You Don't Know How to Sell.

Another way to close effectively is to gain precommitment up front. To do this, establish buying criteria early in the sales cycle. To seek precommitment, you say, "If I can demonstrate today that our [*product/service*] will meet all of the criteria, do we have a basis for doing business?" Then later, after your demonstration, return to the list and say, "We agreed that the following were your top criteria: quality, reliability, cost, and ease of use. And we now agree that we have met your criteria. With your approval, we can begin immediately!"

Also, remember that questions sell. Use them to increase prospect involvement. Use them to probe prospect interests and wants. Use them to probe prospect thoughts and feelings. Use them to allay fears and objections by getting to the roots of prospect concerns. Use them to trial close. Your ability to close depends on your ability to question. A salesperson who sells by questioning sells naturally. And that's sensible selling.

Help Your Customer Win.
Ask for the Sale!

Closes You Can Always Use

 ### The "When Start?" Script

[Mr./Ms. Prospect], now that you see the benefits of our [your product/ service], when would you like [delivery/to get started]?

The "Fit Your Thinking" Script

Does our approach fit your thinking?

The "Add Your Name" Script

Be convincing.

I'd like to add your name to our client list. Shall we move ahead?

The "Win Business" Script

Be sincere.

What do I need to do to win your business?

The "If Roles Reversed?" Script

Put the prospect in your corner.

[*Mr./Ms. Prospect*], if our roles were reversed, what would you do next?

The "Appreciate Benefits" Script

[*Mr./Ms. Prospect*], do you appreciate the many benefits of our [*your product/service*]?

The "If You Proceed?" Script

Soften the close with IF.

If you were to proceed with this purchase, when would you want to start?

The "Situation" Script

Let's take advantage of the situation and make a decision on this today.

The "Problems Vanish" Script

You'd like to have [*productivity/turnover/morale*] problems vanish, wouldn't you?

The "When We Begin to Service" Script

Make the assumption of a sale here.

When we begin to service your account, would you like me to come and introduce it to your people?

The "Reserve a Place" Script

Give the prospect breathing room.

Would you like me to reserve a place for you while we check on the most favorable [*financing/timing*]?

The "Consult" Script

Do you need to consult with anyone else before you [*place an order/ hire us*]?

The "To Your Advantage" Script

If you understood that it was to your advantage to [*own/use*] our [*product/service*] and the terms we worked out were favorable, would you be in a position to proceed today?

The "This Is What You Want" Script

You like what our [*product/service*] will do for you, don't you? Then this is what you want to do the job, isn't it?

The "If I Could Demonstrate?" Script

If I demonstrate that our [*product/service*] could save you and *your company a lot of money, are you in a position to act on it today*?

The "Can You See?" Script

Can you see where this will [*save you money/improve working conditions*]? If you were going to start [*saving/improving*], when do you think would be the best time to begin?

The "I'm Going to Help" Script

Say with confidence:

This is what you need, and I am going to help you get it.

The "Most Important Thing" Script

You told me [*product availability/dependability of service/quality/next day delivery*] is the most important thing to you, is that correct?

If I show you I can provide it, you're prepared to [*give me the order/ hire me and my company*] today—right?

The "Main Concern" Script

What is the main concern you have left?

The "Convince Yourself" Script

Will you please share with me what I would have to do for you to convince yourself to purchase [*your product/service*] today?

The "Delivery" Script

Makes the prospect feel powerful.

How soon would you require delivery?

The "Do Nothing" Script

What happens if you do nothing about the problems you have identified?

The "Our Commitment" Script

Now that you understand our commitment to [*quality/service/state-of-the-art equipment*], can I place your order?

The "Only Thing" Script

If, as you attempt to close, the prospect expresses a concern, try this.

Is this the only thing that stands in the way of your experiencing the value of what we have to offer with our [*your product/service*], or is there something else you need to consider?

If the prospect specifies that this is the only concern, answer the objection in this way.

Have I clarified that point? I want you to know that it was a pleasure to answer that because I understand how happy you are going to be when you discover the value in [*your product/service*].

When would you like to begin enjoying the benefits—[*day*], or is [*another day*] better?

The "Remove Your Concerns" Script

If the prospect identifies several objections that stand in the way, write each down, answer them in turn, and as each is answered to the prospect's satisfaction, say:

I'd now like to remove [*the objection*] as one of your concerns. Is that all right?

Or you can be a bit softer and inquire:

May I now remove the question regarding our [*the objection*]?

Then add:

[*Mr./Ms. Prospect*], I wish everyone I interact with could identify their concerns as easily as you just did. When that occurs, it makes my job fun because it gives me the opportunity to share how good I feel about our [*product/service*] with them. I know you're going to enjoy the benefits our [*product/service*] delivers. Let's take care of the paperwork now.

Obtaining Referrals

Don't Aim Only for a One-Time Run
When You Should Be Planning a Series.
After You Make the First Sale,
Court Your Client and
You'll Also Schedule the Next Sale!

In other words, don't plant annuals when you should be planting perennials. After you make the first sale, plant the seeds for the next sale.

Back to Business Building: The Magic Never Stops

If we're going back to business building, we also have to reconsider how we feel about prospecting. Be honest. Where would you position yourself on the prospecting love-hate continuum?

Prospecting

1	2	3	4	5
Love it				Hate it

Why does prospecting for new sources of business pose problems for salespeople? Why do more sales professionals hate it than love it? For significant numbers of salespeople, prospecting for new business is a hated experience, punctuated with so many painful rejections that the activity literally drives many out of the selling profession. In reality, however, if you want to succeed in sales, prospecting is your umbilical cord. It's your connection to the never-ending body of prospective customers who, once they have the opportunity to hear your story, actually purchase what you're offering. When you prospect, you're looking for qualified buyers who can use your product or service. Although you may have a superb product or service, if you haven't found enough prospects to listen to your story, you won't succeed in bringing in new accounts or in replacing the percentage of existing accounts that you lose due to normal attrition.

The Secret to Business Building Is People.
No Customer Can Be Worse Than NO *Customer.*

No matter where you placed yourself on the love-hate continuum, if you want to stay in sales you have to prospect. You have to make looking for that person who consciously or unconsciously is looking for you a daily activity. The activity will test your endurance, resilience, and motivation to succeed. And it will be just when you want to quit that you'll really need to keep going. Just as exercise conditions your body, prospecting for new business hones your sales acumen. And it must be scheduled into your selling day. Give it up or slack off, and your career turns to flab. Work at it, conquer the sting of rejection, and your career becomes a well-oiled machine. The shape your career is in begins with prospecting. So does the shape of your bankbook. If you are willing to work to build business, you'll end up building your bank account, too. Referrals can help the shape-up process.

Referrals are an underused sales resource. Consider this: You readily recommend restaurants that please you to others. You freely recommend movies you enjoyed to friends and acquaintances. Why wouldn't a satisfied customer be willing to recommend you to someone else who could also use your product or service? It's up to you to leverage the good work you've performed into referrals. It's up to you to transform pleased clients into consistent lead generators.

Lead the Way

In the space provided, identify your top ten customers. Your objective during the next week is to call and obtain at least three leads from each one on your list.

1. _____

2. _____

3. _____

4. _____

5. _____

6. _____

7. _____

8. _____

9. _____

10. _____

It's not only satisfied clients that can serve you up referrals. Sources of referrals are literally unlimited. So get into the world and become a referral detective. Referral givers are "resting" all around you, ready to be awakened by a simple question or request. They may be dining in the restaurant you frequent, or chatting with you at a cocktail party, at the family reunion you didn't want to attend, or on the plane you're taking to a convention. Talk about business with people you meet every day, and people in business will talk about you—and your successes. And that's sensible selling.

Asking for Referrals from Prospects Who Did Not Purchase from You

The "Although You Can't Use" Script

Say courteously:

[*Mr./Ms. Prospect*], although you can't use our [*your product/service*], I'd really appreciate it if you would refer me to those associates or acquaintances who you believe could benefit from it.

The "Who Needs a Good Buy?" Script

[*Mr./Ms. Prospect*], although you can't use our [*your product/ service*], who do you know that is looking for a good buy in [*your product/service*]?

Asking Customers for Referrals

 ### The "Names of Three" Script

Don't be shy. Expect a positive response.

You probably know a number of people who could use our [*your product/service*]. What I'd appreciate is the names of just three of your business acquaintances whom I could call and say that you recommended that I meet with them.

The "Who Would You Call?" Script

Ask the customer to walk in your shoes.

I expect to have the opportunity to visit other people in the area. Maybe you can help me out. If you were me, who would you call on?

The "More Like You" Script

Compliments work here.

[*Mr./Ms. Customer*], I'd love to have more clients like you. Are there any folks you know who you believe would also benefit from using our [*your product/service*]?

The "I'll Write What You Said" Script

This is a great source of the all-important testimonial letter.

[*Mr./Ms. Customer*], the reason you like our [*your product/service*] is because it [*increases profits/builds morale/reduces costs*]. Is that right? I'd sure like to have more satisfied clients like yourself.

How about this? If it's okay with you, I'll jot down what you've just shared with me and send it to you. If what I've written meets with your approval, please ask your secretary to type it on your company's letterhead and then send it back to me. Would you help me build my client base by letting others know how I've helped you to reach your goals?

The "Need Five" Script

Solicit aid from your customer.

[*Mr./Ms. Customer*], I have a problem and I'm hoping you can help me out. I need to find five people who value what you value, who are open to new opportunities, and who might profit from using my [*your product/service*] as you have. Whom do you suggest I contact?

The "Promise Me" (Self-Referral) Script

Say appealingly:

[*Mr./Ms. Customer*], when you think of any other way we may help you or any other service we can provide, promise you'll call me right away.

The "Any Associates" Script

[*Mr./Ms. Customer*], are there any of your associates who would appreciate receiving the same benefits you do from [*your product/ service*]?

EPILOGUE

Epilogue

You are a salesperson. You're in good company. Everybody sells. Some better than others:

> ... Willy was a salesman. And for a salesman there is no rock bottom to the life. He doesn't put a bolt to a nut, he don't tell you the law or give you medicine. He's a man way out there in the blue, riding on a smile and a shoeshine. And when they start not smiling back—that's an earthquake.
>
> Arthur Miller, *Death of a Salesman* (1949)

As Linda, Willy's wife, noted, Willy, the salesman, was "a human being, and a terrible thing is happening to him. So attention must be paid."

This book provides such attention to you, the sales professional. If used properly, it will contribute to sales longevity, not sales demise. It will raise the sales curtain, cue the sales star, and set the stage for sales success.

So remember: You now have all the words, phrases, sentences, and paragraphs you need to influence decision makers and buyers, your co-stars, positively. The practical uses of this resource book will serve you well as you move daily from sales scene to sales scene. With all the scripts in these pages to choose from, your sales activities should repeatedly end in success rather than tragedy. No longer will you be at a loss for words. You'll be able to direct yourself and your career more firmly. You are in the enviable position of having the confidence to share center stage with the prospects you serve. You are in the enviable position of having the confidence to look for sales circumstances that challenge you. And if the circumstances aren't readily available to you right now, you have the know-how to make them available. What's more important, however, is that you can now approach each of these actions, not just by making you and your product look good, but by helping your clients understand how good you and your product will make *them* look. Every prospect wants to be a star, too. Every prospect wants to feel important. Treat your clients like superstars and you'll see magic results.

Sales Scripts That Sell! is your action plan for performance. With it you are ready to sell at a moment's notice, and that's what a successful career in sales requires. This manual gives you the self-discipline of constant preparation, the responses to rejection, and the inner resources to reach the top. With it, the sales show can go on and on. And so can the magic it produces.

Here is your cue book for success. Yes, the show must go on, and yes, you are on call. You need to run toward every opportunity to make a sale. *Sales Scripts That Sell*! Puts this sales know-how at your fingertips. It will also allow you to have fun releasing your sales potential. The magic is now in you. Be sure to pass it on.

INDEX OF SCRIPTS

Index of Scripts

SCRIPTS TO PROSPECT WITH

The "Add to Your Business" Script   45

The "Another Interruption" Script   59

The "Appreciate Thoughtfulness" Script   62

The "Appreciate Your Interest" Script   55

The "Basic" Script   43

The "Better Way" Script   44

The "Boss Will Know Me" Script   57

The "Client of Mine" Script   49

The "Companies Like Yours" Script   47

The "Company's Future" Script   55

The "Company's Interests" Script   63

The "Consider Your Company" Script   65

The "Demonstrate Profits" Script   59

The "Doesn't Interest You" Script   63

The "Economy Is Impacting All Business Today" Script   48

The "Eliminate Words" Script   61

The "Employees Motivated" Script   51

The "Faster to Meet" Script   66

The "Fifteen Minutes" Script   67

The "First and Last Name" Script   54

The "Give You Dollars" Script   46

The "Glad I Found You" Script   50

The "Good Reason" Script   65

The "Has Boss Thanked You?" Script   56

The "Help Me Out" Script   57

The "Help Save" Script   51

The "Higher Profits" Script   48

The "If I Communicated" Script   64

The "If There Were A Way?" Script   56

The "I'm Impressed" Script   62

The "I'm Not Certain" Script   52

The "Important Facts" Script   46

The "Important to Increase" Script   51

The "In Charge" Script   50

The "Increase the Bottom Line" Script   46

The "Increasing" Script   51

The "Interested or Not Interested" Script   66

The "Intrigue" Script   52

The "Invest Minutes" Script   58

The "Just Suppose" Script   56

The "Just Those Words" Script   63

The "Lack of Time" Script   61

The "Leader" Script   45

The "Like to Save" Script   52

The "Make Life Easier" Script   47

The "Materials Needed" Script   54

The "More Important Than Profits" Script   61

The "Most People" Script   52

The "Motivated Employees" Script   61

The "Never Hear That" Script   65

The "Not Today" Script   64

The "On the Line" Script   55

The "Profit Margin" Script   58

The "Prospect Would Want to Know" Script   54

The "Reaction" Script   64

The "Realize Value" Script   58

The "Remind Me" Script   60

The "Same Complaint" Script   61

The "Share an Idea" Script   51

The "Short Presentation" Script   58

The "Sold to Another" Script   44

The "Special Reason" Script   55

The "Still Friends" Script   62

The "Surprises Me" Script   65

The "Takes Longer to Read" Script   60

The "Unfair to Both" Script   67

The "Until I Demonstrate" Script   64

The "Very Busy" Script   60

The "We've Worked For" Script   49

The "What Do You Look For?" Script   44

The "What Interests You?" Script   63

The "Wise Decision" Script   59

The "Working on an Idea" Script   56

The "You'd Be Helping" Script   54

The "You'll Appreciate" Script   52

The "Your Best Customer" Script   59

SCRIPTS THAT HELP CONTROL THE SALE

The "Can You Approve?" Script   77

The "Decide to Buy" Script   75

The "Features and Benefits" Script   77

The "How Long to Approval?" Script   77

The "Key Question" Script   75

The "Learn Needs" Script   75

The "Major Benefits Are" Script   76

The "Next Step" Script   77

The "Other Products" Script   77

The "Prevents" Script   78

The "Someone Else in Decision" Script   78

The "So Special" Script   78

The "Trial Close" Script   78

The "Who Else?" Script   78

SCRIPTS FOR OVERCOMING OBJECTIONS

The "A Year From Now" Script   91

The "Add to Your Business" Script   109

The "Admirable" Script   105

The "Alternative Source" Script   108

The "Apples and Oranges" Script   96

The "Assessment" Script   118

The "Attention to Your Needs" Script   113

The "Attorney or Physician" Script   114

The "Bad Experience" Script   116

The "Change Again" Script   107

The "Change Is Difficult" Script   107

The "Change Is Necessary" Script   107

The "Cheapest" Script   87

The "Compare Competitors" Script   94

The "Compared" Script   118

The "Compared To" Script   88

The "Comparing" Script   85

The "Comparing Us" Script   88

The "Consider Value" Script   85

The "Consultant/Expert" Script   95

The "Convince Yourself" Script   90

The "Cost per Day" Script   92

The "Count on Us" Script   119

The "Daily Cost" Script   88

The "Difficult Decisions" Script   100

The "Disappointments" Script   117

The "Don't Chance Anything" Script   112

The "Doubly Hard" Script   106

The "Easy to Swallow" Script   86

The "Eliminate Options" Script   86

The "Ever Glad?" Script   118

The "Ever Worked With New?" Script   120

The "Explore Possibilities" Script   108

The "Feedback" Script   98

The "Feel and Found" Script   89

The "Get Through" Script   99

The "Give Us a Chance" Script   106

The "Headaches" Script   93

The "High Quality Not Cheap" Script   92

The "How Did You Decide?" Script   109

The "How Many Suppliers?" Script   105

The "I Am Driven" Script   113

The "I Compare Options" Script   95

The "If It Cost Less?" Script   88

The "If Nothing Else" Script   107

The "If Ours Is Better" Script   102

The "If There Were a Way?" Script   109

The "If You Don't" Script   88

The "I'm Not Crazy" Script   115

The "I'm Surprised" Script   104

The "Imitations Versus Original" Script   114

The "Improve the Situation" Script   99

The "Increase Profits" Script   99

The "Initial Advantage" Script   119

The "Invest in Quality" Script   115

The "Invest in the Best" Script   92

The "Is Ours Better?" Script   111

The "Just Like Theirs" Script   110

The "Let's Compare" Script   95

The "Like Giving Up Eating" Script   116

The "Low Price Versus Poor Quality" Script   115

The "Lower Costs" Script   101

The "Make Exceptions?" Script   102

The "Market Share" Script   101

The "Meet the Challenges" Script   100

The "Minimize the Negative" Script   99

The "More Than Fair" Script   90

The "Most Important" Script   112

The "Must Be a Reason" Script   98

The "Need To?" Script   95

The "New" Script   119

The "No Longer Concerned" Script   97

The "Not Asking for All Business" Script   109

The "Not High Enough" Script   88

The "Not Totally Happy?" Script   104

The "Only Money?" Script   89

The "Only Thing?" Script   89

The "Opportunity" Script   105

The "Planning to Pay" Script   86

The "Price and Value" Script   114

The "Price Is Why" Script   86

The "Price or Cost" Script   91

The "Progress" Script   116

The "Quality Concerns You Every Day" Script   90

The "Quality Is Costly" Script   87

The "Recoup" Script   87

The "Resolve the Cost" Script   89

The "Respect Loyalty" Script   102

The "Riskier" Script   118

The "Road of Least Effort" Script   106

The "Second Supplier" Script   112

The "Show You" Script   108

The "Significant Money" Script   86

The "Small Order" Script   105

The "Smart Companies" Script   108

The "Status Quo" Script   107

The "Still Time to Change" Script   97

The "Strong Points" Script   95

The "Their Specifications" Script   94

The "Their Worth" Script   114

The "There Has Been Progress" Script   103

The "They Did Your Homework" Script   94

The "They Know" Script   86

The "They Told Me" Script   106

The "Three Things That Please You" Script   111

The "Times Change" Script   102

The "Today or Ever?" Script   98

The "Tough to Overpay" Script   90

The "Value Is in What It Will Do for You" Script   92

The "Volume Keeps Costs Down" Script   113

The "We Must Determine" Script   112

The "We Took the Best" Script   119

The "We Win the War" Script   91

The "Weather the Storm" Script   100

The "We're Different From" Script   117

The "We're Not Cheap" Script   87

The "We've Grown It" Script   113

The "What Are They Omitting?" Script   115

The "What Caused?" Script   117

The "What Changed?" Script   97

The "What Could Prevent?" Script   94

The "What Do They Do?" Script   105

The "What If We Deserved?" Script   111

The "What Is Keeping You?" Script   104

The "What Makes You?" Script   87

The "Where Did I Go Wrong?" Script   97

The "Who Would?" Script   104

The "Why?" Script   97

The "Why Concerned?" Script   94

The "Why Different?" Script   116

The "Why Hesitating?" Script   89

The "Why They Switched" Script   104

The "Withholding Medicine" Script   100

The "Worth the Change?" Script   102

The "Worth the Trouble?" Script   103

The "Wrong?" Script   116

The "You Deserve Better" Script   103

The "You Were New" Script   120

SCRIPTS FOR HANDLING STALLS

The "Appreciate Honesty" Script   137

The "Best Decision" Script   129

The "Boss Plus" Script   139

The "Competition Plan" Script   135

The "Critical Factors" Script   137

The "Cut Back" Script   134

The "Delay Billing" Script   131

The "Easier Work" Script   128

The "Firm Order" Script   131

The "Great" Script   125

The "Have a Reason" Script   126

The "Holding Back" Script   126

The "Hope to Gain?" Script   132

The "Increase" Script   134

The "Introduce the Boss" Script   138

The "Is Boss Involved?" Script   138

The "Let's Picture" Script   126

The "Lose Competitive Edge" Script   132

The "Main Concern" Script   129

The "Medical Attention" Script   133

The "More Time" Script   126

The "Need to Do" Script   129

The "Needs to Happen" Script   137

The "Not Clearly Communicated" Script   128

The "Not Your Intention" Script   135

The "Paperwork Now" Script   133

The "Persistent Problems" Script   127

The "Phone Call" Script   125

The "Positive Action" Script   135

The "Prevents You" Script   139

The "Prioritize" Script   134

The "Proper Positioning" Script   136

The "Put Heads Together" Script   132

The "Put Off?" Script   131

The "Small Decision" Script   126

The "Small Item" Script   138

The "Special" Script   129

The "Starving" Script   134

The "Take Action" Script   132

The "Talk About" Script   138

The "Testimony" Script   134

The "Thinking Makes Sense" Script   128

The "Think Together" Script   127

The "Think Too Long" Script   128

The "Time and Energy" Script   126

The "Timing Is Important" Script   131

The "Turn Around" Script   135

The "Waiting Costs" Script   135

The "We'll Talk" Script   138

The "What Would It Take?" Script   129

The "Why Delay?" Script   131

The "You Would Not Waste Time" Script   130

The "Your Thinking" Script   137

SCRIPTS THAT LET YOU CLOSE SUCCESSFULLY

The "Add Your Name" Script   147

The "Appreciate Benefits" Script   148

The "Can You See?" Script   149

The "Consult" Script   149

The "Convince Yourself" Script   150

The "Delivery" Script   150

The "Do Nothing" Script   150

The "Fit Your Thinking" Script   147

The "If I Could Demonstrate?" Script   149

The "If Roles Reversed?" Script   148

The "If You Proceed?" Script   148

The "I'm Going to Help" Script   150

The "Main Concern" Script   150

The "Most Important Thing" Script   150

The "Only Thing" Script   150

The "Our Commitment" Script   150

The "Problems Vanish" Script   148

The "Remove Your Concerns" Script   150

The "Reserve a Place" Script   149

The "Situation" Script   148

The "This Is What You Want" Script   149

The "To Your Advantage" Script   149

The "When Start?" Script   147

The "When We Begin to Service" Script   148

The "Win Business" Script   147

SCRIPTS THAT GET YOU REFERRALS

The "Although You Can't Use" Script   157

The "Any Associates" Script   159

The "I'll Write What You Said" Script   158

The "More Like You" Script   158

The "Names of Three" Script   158

The "Need Five" Script   159

The "Promise Me" (Self-Referral) Script   159

The "Who Needs a Good Buy?" Script   157

The "Who Would You Call?" Script   158

Casting Call for More
Sales Scripts That Sell

When the scripts contained in this book either trigger new ideas for you to use in specific selling situations, or prompt you to create personal script variations you want to try out, here's a place to jot them down. Scripts evolve to fit the sales scene—they are not static. We encourage you to grow and treat scripts as part of your daily sales life. Let's face it, attitude is important, but when you step up to the plate, you have to have the words that work.

We'd like to hear your ideas for additional scripts or variations on the ones in this book. You can send them to:

gamble@carroll.com
or
Drs. Teri and Michael Gamble
c/o AMACOM Books
1601 Broadway
New York, New York 10019

_____

_____

_____

_____

About the Authors

Teri Gamble and **Michael Gamble** both have their Ph.D. degrees in Communication from New York University. They are award-winning educators, sales motivators, and trainers, as well as professional speakers. Teri and Mike own their own company—Interact Training Systems—and are the authors of books and articles on sales and communication. One of their books, *Communication Works*, is in its ninth edition. They have taught sales and communication in both corporate training and graduate communication programs. Among the topics they are available to speak to groups on are *The New MEdia Generation, Listen Up!, Understanding Nonverbal Cues and Other Hidden Messages, Harnessing Your Interpersonal Skills, Using Culture as a Guide to Effective Communication,* and *Gender & Communication.*

Teri and Mike have two favorite salespeople: Lindsay, who has her MBA in Marketing and works in real estate recruiting and marketing; and Matthew, a Cell Biologist. They share their home with two toy poodles—Charlie and Lucy.